On
Contentedness
of Mind

AND OTHER MORALIA

Plutarch

On Contentedness of Mind

AND OTHER MORALIA

Introduced by

Ralph Waldo Emerson

LEVENGER PRESS

Published by Levenger Press
420 South Congress Avenue
Delray Beach, Florida 33445 USA
Levengerpress.com

Introduction excerpted from *The Complete Works of Ralph Waldo Emerson: Lectures and Biographical Sketches,* vol. 10, 1884.

Text excerpted from *Plutarch's Morals: Ethical Essays,* translated by Arthur Richard Shilleto, 1898.

Library of Congress Cataloging-in-Publication Data

Plutarch.
  [Moralia. English. Selections]
  On contentedness of mind, and other Moralia / Plutarch ; introduced by Ralph Waldo Emerson.
      p. cm.
  "Text excerpted from Plutarch's Morals: Ethical Essays, translated by Arthur Richard Shilleto, 1898."
  ISBN 978-1-929154-36-4
  1. Greek essays--Translations into English. 2. Ethics--Early works to 1800. I. Emerson, Ralph Waldo, 1803-1882. II. Shilleto, A. R. (Arthur Richard), 1848-1894. III. Title.
  PA4374.M6 2009
  888'.01--dc22

                                2009004332

Cover and book design by Danielle Furci
Mim Harrison, Editor

Printed in the USA

.

CONTENTS

It is a very great indication of progress in virtue to transfer our judgement to action, and not to let our words remain merely words, but to make deeds of them.

Publisher's Preface.

To say there would have been no Shakespeare had there been no Plutarch is an exaggeration, but one with a kernel of truth.

Lucius Mestrius Plutarch was born in Greece in A.D. 46, or thereabouts. He became a biographer, an essayist, and a priest of Apollo at the Oracle of Delphi, appointed to speak for the gods in all manner of human questioning. The Romans, normally a skeptical bunch, considered him a leading thinker of the Empire.

Plutarch is best known for his *Parallel Lives,* a series of two-by-two biographies that profiled one eminent Greek along with an equally illustrious Roman. Cicero, Brutus, Julius Cæsar, Pericles, Demosthenes, and Alexander the Great are among those whose lives he chronicled. As a biographer Plutarch was not one to let facts get in the way; his mission was to convey the overarching moral rather than minutiae. "My intention is not to write histories, but lives," he said, and while *Lives* began as studies of the characters of great men of the age, it became a reference for the study of human nature of any age.

Lives shaped centuries of thought and became the equivalent of a bestseller during the Italian Renaissance. When printed books

became possible, *Lives* was one of the first to go on press—in Rome, fittingly, in 1470.

Sir Thomas North completed the first English translation in 1579, a work that a certain playwright would plumb a few decades later. From *Parallel Lives,* William Shakespeare drew material for his *Antony and Cleopatra, Julius Cæsar,* and *Coriolanus.*

Shakespeare was just one of many to be beguiled by the Delphic observer of the human condition. John Milton, Sir Francis Bacon, the French essayist Montaigne, and the American transcendentalist Emerson all acknowledged a debt to him. "Plutarch always addresses the question on the human side, and not on the metaphysical," Emerson observed.

These essays are Plutarch's oracles on the essence of humanness.

Nowhere is this more evident than in Plutarch's *Moralia,* a series of 78 essays on customs and mores (as *moralia* is often translated). This is the other work for which Plutarch is known, and from which the essays in this book are taken. His topics were wide-reaching—from the education of children and sayings of the Spartan women, to the precepts of statecraft and whether fire or water is more useful.

Plutarch missed Greece's golden ancient age by about five centuries and lived outside its major hubs. Even so, he traveled widely and was often host at his country estate to some of the liveliest thinkers of the day. The earnest conversations that ensued form the basis of *Moralia.* These essays are Plutarch's oracles on the essence of humanness: our weaknesses, desires, needs and strivings. They are studies in the very art and soul of being human, and therein lies their everlasting appeal. What Plutarch never lost, said Emerson, was his wonder. This high priest of the human condition was also everyman, as hopeful as the rest of us.

The *moralia* selected for this work represent the conversations we think Levenger readers would most liked to have joined in at Plutarch's country estate. The language is that of its nineteenth-century translator, the self-described "sometime scholar of Trinity College, Cambridge," Arthur Richard Shilleto. Hence we read "curiosity" where today we would say nosiness, and "shyness" for what we would call timidity. But the moral of each essay still translates—from self-awareness, self-sufficiency and self-control, to finding one's place in the world and making peace with ourselves. It is good to be reminded that others before us have wondered as we still do today.

In his second volume of *Democracy in America* (1840), Alexis de Tocqueville observed that "there is no more wholesome medicine for the mind" than the written works of the Greeks and Romans. Democratic societies in particular "ought frequently to refresh themselves at the springs of ancient literature."

As Americans, we struggle daily with questions of ethics—of *moralia*. As individuals, we can find answers not in Delphic oracles but in the words of thinkers whose wisdom transcends politics and time. And so although twenty centuries have passed, we still find ourselves drawn to the font of Plutarch's wisdom. The wise old Greek speaks to us still.

It is good to be reminded that others before us have wondered as we still do today.

Introduction.

It is remarkable that of an author so familiar as Plutarch, not only to scholars, but to all reading men, and whose history is so easily gathered from his works, no accurate memoir of his life, not even the dates of his birth and death, should have come down to us.

But this neglect by his contemporaries has been compensated by an immense popularity in modern nations. Whilst his books were never known to the world in their own Greek tongue, it is curious that the "Lives" were translated and printed in Latin, thence into Italian, French, and English, more than a century before the original "Works" were yet printed. For whilst the "Lives" were translated in Rome in 1470, and the "Morals," part by part, soon after, the first printed edition of the Greek "Works" did not appear until 1572. Hardly current in his own Greek, these found learned interpreters in the scholars of Germany, Spain and Italy. In France, in the middle of the most turbulent civil wars, Amyot's translation awakened general attention. His genial version of the "Lives" in 1559, of the "Morals" in 1572, had signal success. King Henry IV. wrote to his wife, Marie de Medicis: "*Vive Dieu. As God liveth,* you could not have sent me anything which could be more agreeable than the news of the pleasure you have taken in this reading. Plutarch always delights me with a fresh novelty. To

He had that universal sympathy with genius which makes all its victories his own.

love him is to love me; for he has been long time the instructor of my youth. My good mother, to whom I owe all, and who would not wish, she said, to see her son an illustrious dunce, put this book into my hands almost when I was a child at the breast. It has been like my conscience, and has whispered in my ear many good suggestions and maxims for my conduct and the government of my affairs." Still earlier, Rabelais cites him with due respect. Montaigne, in 1589, says: "We dunces had been lost, had not this book raised us out of the dirt. By this favor of his we dare now speak and write. The ladies are able to read to schoolmasters. 'Tis our breviary." Montesquieu drew from him his definition of law, and, in his Pensees, declares, "I am always charmed with Plutarch; in his writings are circumstances attached to persons, which give great pleasure;" and adds examples. Saint Evremond read Plutarch to the great Conde under a tent. Rollin, so long the historian of antiquity for France, drew unhesitatingly his history from him. Voltaire honored him, and Rousseau acknowledged him as his master. In England, Sir Thomas North translated the "Lives" in 1579, and Holland the "Morals" in 1603, in time to be used by Shakspeare in his plays, and read by Bacon, Dryden, and Cudworth.

Plutarch occupies a unique place in literature as an encyclopædia of Greek and Roman antiquity. Whatever is eminent in fact or in fiction, in opinion, in character, in institutions, in science— natural, moral, or metaphysical, or in memorable sayings, drew his attention and came to his pen with more or less fulness of record. He is, among prose writers, what Chaucer is among English poets, a repertory for those who want the story without searching for it at first hand,—a compend of all accepted traditions. And all this without any supreme intellectual gifts. He is not a profound mind; not a master in any science; not a lawgiver, like Lycurgus or Solon; not a metaphysician, like Parmenides, Plato, or Aristotle; not the founder of any sect or community, like Pythagoras or Zeno: not a naturalist, like Pliny or Linnæus; not a leader of the mind of a generation, like Plato or Goethe. But if he had not the highest powers, he was yet a man of rare gifts. He had that universal sympathy with genius which makes all its victories his own; though he never used verse, he had many qualities of the poet in the power of his imagination, the speed of his mental associations, and his sharp, objective eyes. But what specially marks him, he is a chief example of the illumination of the intellect by the force of morals. Though the most amiable of boon-companions, this generous religion gives him *apercus* like Goethe's.

Plutarch was well-born, well-taught, well-conditioned: a self-respecting, amiable man, who knew how to better a good education by travels, by devotion to affairs private and public; a master of ancient culture, he read books with a just criticism; eminently social, he was a king in his own house, surrounded himself with select friends, and knew the high value of good conversation; and declares in a letter written to his wife that he finds scarcely an erasure, as in a book well-written, in the happiness of his life.

The range of mind makes the glad writer. The reason of Plutarch's vast popularity is his humanity. A man of society, of affairs; upright, practical; a good son, husband, father, and friend,—he has a taste for common life, and knows the court, the camp and the judgment-hall, but also the forge, farm, kitchen and cellar, and every utensil and use, and with a wise man's or a poet's eye. Thought defends him from any degradation. He does not lose his way, for the attractions are from within, not from without.

Plutarch declares in a letter written to his wife that he finds scarcely an erasure, as in a book well-written, in the happiness of his life.

A poet in verse or prose must have a sensuous eye, but an intellectual co-perception. Plutarch's memory is full, and his horizon wide. Nothing touches man but he feels to be his; he is tolerant even of vice, if he finds it genial; enough a man of the world to give even the Devil his due, and would have hugged Robert Burns, when he cried:—

"O wad ye tak' a thought and mend!"

He is a philosopher with philosophers, a naturalist with naturalists, and sufficiently a mathematician to leave some of his readers, now and then, at a long distance behind him, or respectfully skipping to the next chapter. But this scholastic omniscience of our author engages a new respect, since they hope he understands his own diagram.

He perpetually suggests Montaigne, who was the best reader he has ever found, though Montaigne excelled his master in the point and surprise of his sentences. Plutarch had a religion which Montaigne wanted, and which defends him from wantonness; and though Plutarch is as plain-spoken, his moral sentiment is always pure. What better praise has any writer received than he whom Montaigne finds "frank in giving things, not words," dryly adding, "it vexes me that he is so exposed to the spoil of those that are conversant with him." It is one of the felicities of literary history, the tie which inseparably couples these two names across fourteen centuries. Montaigne, whilst he grasps Etienne de la Boece with one hand, reaches back the other to Plutarch. These distant friendships charm us, and honor all the parties, and make the best example of the universal citizenship and fraternity of the human mind.

His sharp objective eyes see everything that moves, shines, or threatens in thought or dreams.

I do not know where to find a book—to borrow a phrase of Ben Jonson's—"so rammed with life," and this in chapters chiefly ethical, which are so prone to be heavy and sentimental. No poet could illustrate his thought with more novel or striking similes or happier anecdotes. His style is realistic, picturesque and varied; his sharp objective eyes seeing everything that moves, shines, or threatens in nature or art, or thought or dreams. Indeed, twilights, shadows, omens and spectres have a charm for him. He believes in witchcraft and the evil eye, in demons and ghosts,— but prefers, if you please, to talk of these in the morning. His vivacity and abundance never leave him to loiter or pound on an incident. I admire his rapid and crowded style, as if he had such store of anecdotes of his heroes that he is forced to suppress more than he recounts, in order to keep up with the hasting history.

His surprising merit is the genial facility with which he deals with his manifold topics. There is no trace of labor or pain. He gossips of heroes, philosophers and poets; of virtues and genius; of love and fate and empires. It is for his pleasure that he recites all that is best in his reading: he prattles history. But he is no courtier, and no Boswell: he is ever manly, far from fawning, and would be welcome to the sages and warriors he reports, as one having a native right to admire and recount these stirring deeds and speeches. His superstitions are poetic, aspiring, affirmative.
A poet might rhyme all day with hints drawn from Plutarch, page on page. No doubt, this superior suggestion for the modern reader owes much to the foreign air, the Greek wine, the religion and history of antique heroes. Thebes, Sparta, Athens and Rome charm us away from the disgust of the passing hoar. But his own cheerfulness and rude health are also magnetic. In his immense quotation and allusion we quickly cease to discriminate between what he quotes and what he invents. We sail on his memory into

He has preserved for us a multitude of precious sentences, in prose or verse, of authors whose books are lost.

the ports of every nation, enter into every private property, and do not stop to discriminate owners, but give him the praise of all. 'Tis all Plutarch, by right of eminent domain, and all property vests in this emperor. This facility and abundance make the joy of his narrative, and he is read to the neglect of more careful historians. Yet he inspires a curiosity, sometimes makes a necessity, to read them. He disowns any attempt to rival Thucydides; but I suppose he has a hundred readers where Thucydides finds one, and Thucydides must often thank Plutarch for that one. He has preserved for us a multitude of precious sentences, in prose or verse, of authors whose books are lost; and these embalmed fragments, through his loving selection alone, have come to be proverbs of later mankind.

Plutarch thought it the top of wisdom to philosophize yet not appear to do it.

'Tis almost inevitable to compare Plutarch with Seneca, who, born fifty years earlier, was for many years his contemporary, though they never met, and their writings were perhaps unknown to each other. Plutarch is genial, with an endless interest in all human and divine things; Seneca, a professional philosopher, a writer of sentences, and, though he keep a sublime path, is less interesting, because less humane; and when we have shut his book, we forget to open it again. There is a certain violence in his opinions, and want of sweetness. He lacks the sympathy of Plutarch. He is tiresome through perpetual didactics. He is not happily living. Cannot the simple lover of truth enjoy the virtues of those he meets, and the virtues suggested by them, so to find himself at some time purely contented? Seneca was still more a man of the world than Plutarch; and, by his conversation with the Court of Nero, and his own skill, like Voltaire's, of living with men of business and emulating their address in affairs by great accumulation of his own property, learned to temper his philosophy with facts. He ventured far,—apparently too far,—for so keen a conscience as he inly had. Yet we owe to that wonderful moralist illustrious maxims; as if the scarlet vices of the times of Nero had the natural effect of driving virtue to its loftiest antagonisms. "Seneca," says L'Estrange, "was a pagan Christian, and is very good reading for our Christian pagans." He was Buddhist in his cold abstract virtue, with a certain impassibility beyond humanity. He called pity, "that fault of narrow souls." Yet what noble words we owe to him: "God divided man into men, that they might help each other;" and again, "The good man differs from God in nothing but duration." His thoughts are excellent, if only he had the right to say them. Plutarch, meantime, with every virtue under heaven, thought it the top of wisdom to philosophize yet not appear to do it, and to reach in mirth the same ends which the most serious are proposing.

Plutarch's popularity will return in rapid cycles. If over-read in this decade, so that his anecdotes and opinions become commonplace, and today's novelties are sought for variety, his sterling values will presently recall the eye and thought of the best minds, and his books will be reprinted and read anew by coming generations. And thus Plutarch will be perpetually rediscovered from time to time as long as books last.

— *Ralph Waldo Emerson*
1884

Plutarch will be perpetually rediscovered as long as books last.

How a Man May Be Benefited By His Enemies.

I am well aware, Cornelius Pulcher, that you prefer the mildest manners in public life, by which you can be at once most useful to the community, and most agreeable in private life to those who have any dealings with you. But since it is difficult to find any region without wild beasts, though it is related of Crete; and hitherto there has been no state that has not suffered from envy, rivalry, and strife, the most fruitful seeds of hostility; (for, even if nothing else does, our friendships involve us in enmities, as Chilo the wise man perceived, who asked the man who told him he had no enemy, whether he had a friend either), it seems to me that a public man ought not only to examine the whole question of enemies in its various ramifications, but also to listen to the serious remark of Xenophon, that a sensible man will receive profit even from his enemies. The ideas therefore that lately occurred to me to deliver, I have now put together nearly in the identical words and send them to you, with the exception of some matter also in "Political Precepts," a treatise which I have often noticed in your hands.

II. People in old times were well satisfied if they were not injured by strange and wild beasts, and that was the only motive of their

fights with them, but those of later days have by now learnt to make use of them, for they feed on their flesh, and clothe themselves with their wool, and make medical use of their gall and beestings, and turn their hides into shields, so that we might reasonably fear, if beasts failed man, that his life would become brutish, and wild, and void of resources. Similarly since all others are satisfied with not being injured by their enemies, but the sensible will also (as Xenophon says) get profit out of them, we must not be incredulous, but seek a method and plan how to obtain this advantage, seeing that life without an enemy is impossible. The husbandman cannot cultivate every tree, nor can the hunter tame every kind of animal, so both seek means to derive profit according to their several necessities, the one from his barren trees, the other from his wild animals. Sea-water also is undrinkable and brackish, but it feeds fish, and is a sort of vehicle to convey and transport travellers anywhere. The Satyr, when he saw fire for the first time, wished to kiss it and embrace it, but Prometheus warned him,

The enemy gives us a handle to make use of him by, and so is serviceable.

> *"Goat, thou wilt surely mourn thy loss of beard."*

For fire burns whoever touches it, but it also gives light and warmth, and is an instrument of art to all those who know how to use it. Consider also in the case of the enemy, if he is in other respects injurious and intractable, he somehow or other gives us a handle to make use of him by, and so is serviceable. And many things are unpleasant and detestable and antagonistic to those to whom they happen, but you must have noticed that some use even illnesses as a period of rest for the body, and others by excessive toil have strengthened and trained their bodily vigour, and some have made exile and the loss of money a passage to leisure and philosophy, as did Diogenes and Crates. And Zeno, when he heard of the wreck of the ship which contained all his property, said, "Thou hast done well, Fortune, to confine me to my threadbare cloak."

For as those animals that have the strongest and healthiest stomachs eat and digest serpents and scorpions, and some even feed on stones and shells, which they convert into nourishment by the strength and heat of their stomachs, while fastidious people out of health almost vomit if offered bread and wine, so foolish people spoil even their friendships, while the wise know how to turn to account even their enmities.

III. In the first place then it seems to me that what is most injurious in enmity may become most useful to those that pay attention to it. To what do I refer? Why, to the way in which your enemy ever wide awake pries into all your affairs, and analyzes your whole life, trying to get a handle against you somewhere, able not only to look through a tree, like Lynceus, or through stones and shells, but through your friend and domestic and every intimate acquaintance, as far as possible detecting your doings, and digging and ferreting into your designs. For our friends are ill and often die without our knowing anything about it through our delay and carelessness, but we almost pry into even the dreams of our enemies; and our enemy knows even more than we do ourselves of our diseases and debts and differences with our wives. But they pay most attention to our faults and hunt them out: and as vultures follow the scent of putrid carcases, and cannot perceive sound and wholesome ones, so the diseases and vices and crimes of life attract the enemy, and on these those that hate us pounce, these they attack and tear to pieces. Is not this an advantage to us? Certainly it is. For it teaches us to live warily and be on our guard, and neither to do or say anything carelessly or without

What is most injurious in enmity may become most useful to those that pay attention to it.

3

"How shall I avenge myself on my enemy?" "By becoming a good and honest man."

circumspection, but ever to be vigilant by careful mode of living that we give no handle to an enemy. For the cautiousness that thus represses the passions and follows reason implants a care and determination to live well and without reproach. For as those states that have been sobered by wars with their neighbours and continual campaigns love the blessings of order and peace, so those people who are compelled to lead a sober life owing to their enemies, and to be on their guard against carelessness and negligence, and to do everything with an eye to utility, imperceptibly glide into a faultless mode of life, and tone down their character, even without requiring much assistance from precepts. For those who always remember the line,

"Ah! how would Priam and his sons rejoice,"

are by it diverted from and learn to shun all such things as their enemies would rejoice and laugh at. Again we see actors and singers on the stage oftentimes slack and remiss, and not taking sufficient pains about their performances in the theatres when they have it all to themselves; but when there is a competition and contest with others, they not only wake up but tune their instruments, and adjust their chords, and play on the flute with more care. Similarly whoever knows that his enemy is antagonistic to his life and character, pays more attention to himself, and watches his behaviour more carefully, and regulates his life. For it is peculiar to vice to be more afraid of enemies than friends in regard to our faults. And so Nasica, when some expressed their opinion that the Roman Republic was now secure, since Carthage was rased to the ground and Achaia reduced to slavery, said, "Nay rather we are now in a critical position, since we have none left to fear or respect."

IV. Consider also that very philosophical and witty answer of Diogenes to the man who asked, "How shall I avenge myself on my enemy?" "By becoming a good and honest man." Some people are terribly put about if they see their enemies' horses in a good condition, or hear their dogs praised; if they see their farm well-tilled, their garden well-kept, they groan aloud. What a state think you then they would be in, if you were to exhibit yourself as a just man, sensible and good, in words excellent, in deeds pure, in manner of life decorous, "reaping fruit from the deep soil of the soul, where good counsels grow." Pindar says "those that are conquered are reduced to complete silence:" but not absolutely, not all men, only those that see they are outdone by their enemies in industry, in goodness, in magnanimity, in humanity, in kindnesses; these, as Demosthenes says, "stop the tongue, block up the mouth, choke people, and make them silent."

"Be better than the bad: 'tis in your power."

If you wish to vex the man who hates you, do not abuse him by calling him a pathick, or effeminate, or intemperate, or a low fellow, or illiberal; but be yourself a man, and temperate, and truthful, and kind and just in all your dealings with those you come across. But if you are tempted to use abuse, mind that you yourself are very far from what you abuse him for, dive down into your own soul, look for any rottenness in yourself, lest someone suggest to you the line of the tragedian,

"You doctor others, all diseased yourself."

If you say your enemy is uneducated, increase your own love of learning and industry; if you call him coward, stir up the more your own spirit and manliness; and if you say he is wanton and

If you say your enemy is uneducated, increase your own love of learning; if you call him coward, stir up the more your own spirit.

licentious, erase from your own soul any secret trace of the love of pleasure. For nothing is more disgraceful or more unpleasant than slander that recoils on the person who sets it in motion; for as the reflection of light seems most to injure weak eyes, so does censure when it recoils on the censurer, and is borne out by the facts. For as the north-east wind attracts clouds, so does a bad life draw upon itself rebukes.

V. Whenever Plato was in company with people who behaved in an unseemly manner, he used to say to himself, "Am I such a person as this?" So he that censures another man's life, if he straightway examines and mends his own, directing and turning it into the contrary direction, will get some advantage from his censure, which will be otherwise idle and unprofitable. Most people laugh if a bald-pate or hump-back jeer and mock at others who are so too: it is quite as ridiculous to jeer and mock if one lies open to retort oneself, as Leo of Byzantium showed in his answer to the hump-back who jeered at him for weakness of eyes, "You twit me with an infirmity natural to man, while you yourself carry your Nemesis on your back." And so do not abuse another as an adulterer, if you yourself are mad after boys: nor as a spendthrift, if you yourself are niggardly. Alcmæon said to Adrastus, "You are near kinsman to a woman that slew her husband." What was his reply? He retaliated on him with the appropriate retort, "But you killed with your own hand the mother that bore you." And Domitius said to Crassus, "Did you not weep for the lamprey that was bred in your fishpond, and died?" To which Crassus replied, "Did you weep, when you buried your three wives?" He therefore that intends to abuse others must not be witty and noisy and impudent, but a man that does not lie open to counter-abuse and retort, for the god seems to have enjoined upon no one the precept "Know thyself" so much as on the person who is

As the north-east wind attracts clouds, so does a bad life draw upon itself rebukes.

censorious, to prevent people saying just what they please, and hearing what don't please them. For such a one is wont, as Sophocles says, "idly letting his tongue flow, to hear against his will, what he willingly says ill of others."

VI. This use and advantage then there is in abusing one's enemy, and no less arises from being abused and ill-spoken of oneself by one's enemies. And so Antisthenes said well that those who wish to lead a good life ought to have genuine friends or red-hot enemies; for the former deterred you from what was wrong by reproof, the latter by abuse. But since friendship has nowadays become very mealy-mouthed in freedom of speech, voluble in flattery and silent in rebuke, we can only hear the truth from our enemies. For as Telephus having no surgeon of his own, submitted his wound to be cured by his enemy's spear, so those who cannot procure friendly rebuke must content themselves with the censure of an enemy that hates them, reprehending and castigating their vices, and regard not the animus of the person, but only his matter. For as he who intended to kill the Thessalian Prometheus only stabbed a tumour, and so lanced it that the man's life was saved, and he was rid of the tumour by its bursting, so oftentimes abuse, suddenly thrust on a man in anger or hatred, has cured some disease in his soul which he was ignorant of or neglected. But most people when they are abused do not consider whether the abuse really belongs to them properly, but look round to see what abuse they can heap on the abuser, and, as wrestlers get smothered with the dust of the arena, do not wipe off the abuse hurled at themselves, but bespatter others, and at last get on both sides grimy and discoloured. But if anyone gets a bad name from an enemy, he ought to clear himself of the imputation even more than he would remove any stain on his clothes that was pointed out to him; and if it be wholly untrue, yet he ought to investigate

Those who wish to lead a good life ought to have genuine friends or red-hot enemies; for the former deterred you from what was wrong by reproof, the latter by abuse.

what originated the charge, and to be on his guard and be afraid lest he had unawares done something very near akin to what was imputed to him. As Lacydes, the king of the Argives, by the way he wore his hair and by his mincing walk got charged with effeminacy: and Pompey's scratching his head with one finger was construed in the same way, though both these men were very far from effeminacy or wantonness. And Crassus was accused of an intrigue with one of the Vestal Virgins, because he wished to purchase from her a pleasant estate, and therefore frequently visited her and waited upon her. And Postumia, from her readiness to laugh and talk somewhat freely with men, got accused and even had to stand her trial for incest, but was, however, acquitted of that charge: but Spurius Minucius the Pontif ex Maximus, when he pronounced her innocent, urged her not to be freer in her words than she was in her life. And though Themistocles was guiltless of treason, his intimacy with Pausanias, and the letters and messages that frequently passed between them, laid him under suspicion.

Whenever any false charge is made against us, we ought to see what word or action has made the charge seem probable.

VII. Whenever therefore any false charge is made against us, we ought not merely to despise and neglect it as false, but to see what word or action, either in jest or earnest, has made the charge seem probable, and this we must for the future be earnestly on our guard against and shun. For if others falling into unforeseen trouble and difficulties teach us what is expedient, as Merope says,

"Fortune has made me wise, though she has ta'en
My dearest ones as wages,"

why should we not take an enemy, and pay him no wages, to teach us, and give us profit and instruction, in matters which had escaped our notice? For an enemy has keener perception than a friend, for, as Plato says, "the lover is blind as respects the loved one," and hatred is both curious and talkative. Hiero was twitted by one of his enemies for his foul breath, so he went home and said to his wife, "How is this? You never told me of it." But she being chaste and innocent replied, "I thought all men's breath was like that." Thus perceptible and material things, and things that are plain to everybody, are sooner learnt from enemies than from friends and intimates.

VIII. Moreover to keep the tongue well under control, no small factor in moral excellence, and to make it always obedient and submissive to reason, is not possible, unless by practice and attention and painstaking a man has subdued his worst passions, as for example anger. For such expressions as "a word uttered involuntarily," and "escaping the barrier of the teeth," and "words darting forth spontaneously," well illustrate what happens in the case of ill-disciplined souls, ever wavering and in an unsettled condition through infirmity of temper, through unbridled fancy, or through faulty education. But, according to divine Plato, though a word seems a very trivial matter, the heaviest penalty follows upon it both from gods and men. But silence can never be called to account, is not only not thirsty, to borrow the language of Hippocrates, but when abused is dignified and Socratic, or rather Herculean, if indeed it was Hercules who said,

> *"Sharp words he heeded not so much as flies."*

Not more dignified and noble than this is it to keep silent when an enemy reviles you, "as one swims by a smooth and mocking cliff," but in practice it is better. If you accustom yourself to bear silently the abuse of an enemy, you will very easily bear the attack of a scolding wife, and will remain undisturbed when you hear the

Keep the tongue well under control, no small factor in moral excellence, and make it always obedient and submissive to reason.

9

We should accustom ourselves to deal justly even with our enemies, and then there will be no fear that we should ever act unjustly to our friends.

sharp language of a friend or brother, and will be calm and placid when you are beaten or have something thrown at your head by your father or mother. For Socrates put up with Xanthippe, a passionate and forward woman, which made him a more easy companion with others, as being accustomed to submit to her caprices; and it is far better to train and accustom the temper to bear quietly the insults and rages and jeers and taunts of enemies and estranged persons, and not to be distressed at it.

IX. Thus then must we exhibit in our enmities meekness and forbearance, and in our friendships still more simplicity and magnanimity and kindness. For it is not so graceful to do a friend a service, as disgraceful to refuse to do so at his request; and not to revenge oneself on an enemy when opportunity offers is generous. But the man who sympathizes with his enemy in affliction, and assists him in distress, and readily holds out a helping hand to his children and family and their fortunes when in a low condition, whoever does not admire such a man for his humanity, and praise his benevolence,

"He has a black heart made of adamant
Or iron or bronze."

When Cæsar ordered the statues of Pompey that had been thrown down to be put up again, Cicero said, "You have set up again Pompey's statues, and in so doing have erected statues to yourself." We ought not therefore to be niggardly in our praise and honour of an enemy that deserves a good name. For he who praises another receives on that account greater praise himself, and is the more credited on another occasion when he finds fault, as not having any personal ill-feeling against the man, but only disapproving of his act; and what is most noble and advantageous, the man who is accustomed to praise his enemies, and not to be vexed or malignant at their prosperity, is as far as possible from envying the good fortune of his friends, and the success of his intimates. And yet what practice will be more beneficial to our minds, or bring about a happier disposition, than that which banishes from us all jealousy and envy? For as in war many necessary things, otherwise bad, are customary and have as it were the sanction of law, so that they cannot be abolished in spite of the injury they do, so enmity drags along in its train hatred, and envy, and jealousy, and malignity, and revenge, and stamps them on the character. Moreover knavery, and deceit, and villainy, that seem neither bad nor unfair if employed against an enemy, if they once get planted in the mind are difficult to dislodge; and eventually from force of habit get used also against friends, unless they are forewarned and forearmed through their previous acquaintance with the tricks of enemies. If then Pythagoras, accustoming his disciples to abstain from all cruelty and inhumanity to the brute creation, did right to discountenance bird-fowling, and to buy up draughts of fishes and bid them be thrown into the water again, and to forbid killing any but wild animals, much more noble is it, in dissensions and differences with human beings, to be a generous, just and true enemy, and to check and tame all bad and low and knavish propensities, that in all intercourse with friends a man may keep the peace and abstain from doing an injury. Scaurus was an enemy and accuser of Domitius, but when one of Domitius' slaves came to him to reveal some important matters which were unknown to Scaurus, he would not hear him, but seized him and sent him back to his master. And when Cato was prosecuting Murena for canvassing, and was getting together his evidence, he was accompanied as was usual by people who watched what he was doing, and would often ask him if he intended that day to get together his witnesses and open the case,

Let us be rivals of our enemies for glory or office or righteous gain, trying to outdo them in industry, and hard work, and soberness, and prudence.

and if he said "No," they believed him and went their way. All this is the greatest proof of the credit which was reposed in Cato, but it is better and more important, that we should accustom ourselves to deal justly even with our enemies, and then there will be no fear that we should ever act unjustly and treacherously to our friends and intimates.

X. But since, as Simonides says, "all larks must have their crests," and every man's nature contains in it pugnacity and jealousy and envy, which last is, as Pindar says, "the companion of empty-headed men," one might get considerable advantage by purging oneself of those passions against enemies, and by diverting them, like sewers, as far as possible from companions and friends. And this it seems the statesmanlike Onomademus had remarked, for being on the victorious side in a disturbance at Chios, he urged his party not to expel all of the different faction, but to leave some, "in order," he said, "that we may not begin to quarrel with our friends, when we have got entirely rid of our enemies." So too our expending these passions entirely on our enemies will give less trouble to our friends. For it ought not to be, as Hesiod says, that "potter envies potter, and singer envies singer, and neighbour neighbour," and cousin cousin, and brother brother, "if hastening to get rich" and enjoying prosperity. But if there is no other way to get rid of strife and envy and quarrels, accustom yourself to be vexed at your enemies' good fortune, and sharpen and accentuate on them your acerbity. For as judicious gardeners think they produce finer roses and violets by planting alongside of them garlic and onions, that any bitter or strong elements may be transferred to them, so your enemy's getting and attracting your envy and malignity will render you kinder and more agreeable to your prosperous friends. And so let us be rivals of our enemies for glory or office or righteous gain, not only being

As Plato says, "all the gold above or below the earth is not of equal value with virtue."

vexed if they get ahead of us, but also carefully observing all the steps by which they get ahead, and trying to outdo them in industry, and hard work, and soberness, and prudence; as Themistocles said Miltiades' victory at Marathon would not let him sleep. For he who thinks his enemy gets before him in offices, or advocacies, or state affairs, or in favour with his friends or great men, if from action and emulation he sinks into envy and despondency, makes his life become idle and inoperative. But he who is not blinded by hate, but a discerning spectator of life and character and words and deeds, will perceive that most of what he envies comes to those who have them from diligence and prudence and good actions, and exerting himself in the same direction he will increase his love of what is honourable and noble, and will eradicate his vanity and sloth.

XI. But if our enemies seem to us to have got either by flattery, or fraud, or bribery, or venal services, ill-got and discreditable power at court or in state, it ought not to trouble us but rather inspire pleasure in us, when we compare our own liberty and purity and independence of life. For, as Plato says, "all the gold above or below the earth is not of equal value with virtue." And we ought ever to remember the precept of Solon, "We will not exchange our virtue for others' wealth." Nor will we give up our virtue for the applause of banqueting theatres, nor for honours and chief seats among eunuchs and harlots, nor to be monarchs' satraps; for nothing is to be desired or noble that comes from what is bad. But since, as Plato says, "the lover is blind as respects the loved one," and we notice more what our enemies do amiss, we ought not to let either our joy at their faults or our grief at their success be idle, but in either case we ought to reflect, how we may become better than them by avoiding their errors, and by imitating their virtues not come short of them.

Nothing is to be desired or noble that comes from what is bad.

13

ON TALKATIVENESS.

P hilosophy finds talkativeness a disease very difficult and hard to cure. For its remedy, conversation, requires hearers: but talkative people hear nobody, for they are ever prating. And the first evil this inability to keep silence produces is an inability to listen. It is a self-chosen deafness of people who, I take it, blame nature for giving us one tongue and two ears. If then the following advice of Euripides to a foolish hearer was good,

> *"I cannot fill one that can nought retain,*
> *Pumping up wise words for an unwise man;"*

one might more justly say to a talkative man, or rather about a talkative man,

> *"I cannot fill one that will nothing take,*
> *Pumping up wise words for an unwise man;"*

or rather deluging with words one that talks to those who don't listen, and listens not to those who talk. Even if he does listen for a short time, talkativeness hurries off what is said like the retiring sea, and anon brings it up again multiplied with the approaching tide. The portico at Olympia that returns many echoes to one

utterance is called seven-voiced, and if the slightest utterance catches the ear of talkativeness, it at once echoes it all round,

"Moving the mind's chords all unmoved before."

For their ears can certainly have no passages leading to the brain but only to the tongue. And so while other people retain what they hear, talkative people lose it altogether, and, being empty-headed, they resemble empty vessels, and go about making much noise.

"Is not this wonderful, Aristotle?" "Not at all," said he, "but it is wonderful that anyone with a pair of legs stops here to listen to you."

II. If however it seems that no attempt at cure has been left untried, let us say to the talkative person,

"Be silent, boy; silence has great advantages;"

two of the first and foremost of which are hearing and being heard, neither of which can happen to talkative people, for however they desire either so unhappy are they that they must desist from it. For in all other diseases of the soul, as love of money, love of glory, or love of pleasure, people at any rate attain the desired object: but it is the cruel fate of talkative people to desire hearers but not to get them, for everyone flees from them with headlong speed; and if people are sitting or walking about in any public place, and see one coming they quickly pass the word to one another to shift quarters. And as when there is dead silence in any assembly they say Hermes has joined the company, so when any prater joins some drinking party or social gathering of friends, all are silent, not wishing to give him a chance to break in, and if he uninvited begin to open his mouth, they all, "like before a storm at sea, when Boreas is blowing a gale round some headland," foreseeing tossing about and nausea, disperse. And so it is their destiny to find neither willing table-companions, nor messmates when they are travelling by land or by sea, but only such as cannot help themselves; for such a fellow is always at you, plucking hold of your clothes or chin, or giving you a dig in the ribs with his elbow. "Most valuable are the feet in such a conjuncture," according to Archilochus, nay according to the wise Aristotle himself. For he being bothered with a talkative fellow, and wearied out with his absurd tales, and his frequent question, "Is not this wonderful, Aristotle?" "Not at all," said he, "but it is wonderful that anyone with a pair of legs stops here to listen to you." And to another such fellow, who said after a long rigmarole, "Did I weary you, philosopher, by my chatter?" "Not you, by Zeus," said he, "for I paid no attention to you." For even if talkative people force you to listen, the mind can give them only its outward ears to deluge, while it unfolds and pursues some other thoughts within; so they find neither hearers to attend to them, nor credit them. They say those that are prone to Venus are commonly barren: so the prating of talkative people is ineffectual and fruitless.

III. And yet nature has fenced and barricaded in us nothing so much as the tongue, having put the teeth before it as a barrier, so that if, when reason holds tight her "glossy reins," it hearken not, nor keep within bounds, we may check its intemperance, biting it till the blood comes. For Euripides tells us that, not from unbolted houses or store-rooms, but "from unbridled mouths the end is misfortune." But those persons who think that houses without doors and open purses are no good to their possessors, and yet keep their mouths open and unshut, and allow their speech to flow continually like the waves of the Euxine, seem to regard speech as of less value than anything. And so they never get believed, though credit is the aim of every speech; for to inspire belief in one's hearers is the proper end of speech, but praters are

Nature has fenced and barricaded in us nothing so much as the tongue, having put the teeth before it as a barrier.

Praters are disbelieved even when they tell the truth.

disbelieved even when they tell the truth. For as corn stowed away in a granary is found to be larger in quantity but inferior in quality, so the speech of a talkative man is increased by a large addition of falsehood, which destroys his credit.

IV. Then again every man of modesty and propriety would avoid drunkenness, for anger is next door neighbour to madness as some think, but drunkenness lives in the same house: or rather drunkenness is madness, more short-lived indeed, but more potent also through volition, for it is self-chosen. Nor is drunkenness censured for anything so much as its intemperate and endless talk.

> "Wine makes a prudent man begin to sing,
> And gently laugh, and even makes him dance."

And yet there is no harm in all this, in singing and laughing and dancing. But the poet adds—

> "And it compels to say what's best unsaid."

This is indeed dreadful and dangerous. And perhaps the poet in this passage has solved that problem of the philosophers, and stated the difference between being under the influence of wine and being drunk, mirth being the condition of the former, foolish talk of the latter. For as the proverb tells us, "What is in the heart of the sober is on the tongue of the drunken." And so Bias, being silent at a drinking bout, and jeered at by some young man in the company as stupid, replied, "What fool could hold his tongue in liquor?" And at Athens a certain person gave an entertainment to the king's ambassadors, and at their desire contrived to get the philosophers there too, and as they were all talking together and comparing ideas, and Zeno alone was silent, the strangers greeted him and pledged him, and said, "What are we to tell the king about you, Zeno?" And he replied, "Nothing, but that there is an old man at Athens that can hold his tongue at a drinking bout." So profound and mysterious and sober is silence, while drunkenness is talkative: for it is void of sense and understanding, and so is loquacious. And so the philosophers define drunkenness to be silly talk in wine. Drinking therefore is not censured, if silence go with it, but foolish prating turns being under the influence of wine into drunkenness. And the drunken man prates only in his cups; but the talkative man prates everywhere, in the market-place, in the theatre, out walking, by night and by day. If he is your doctor, he is more trouble to you than your disease: if he is on board ship with you, he disgusts you more than sea-sickness; if he praises you, he is more fulsome than blame. It is more pleasure associating with bad men who have tact than with good men who prate. Nestor indeed in Sophocles' Play, trying by his words to soothe exasperated Ajax, said to him mildly,

> *"I blame you not, for though your words are bad,*
> *Your acts are good:"*

but we cannot feel so to the talkative man, for his want of tact in words destroys and undoes all the grace of his actions.

V. Lysias wrote a defence for some accused person, and gave it him, and he read it several times, and came to Lysias in great dejection and said, "When I first perused this defence, it seemed to me wonderful, but when I read it a second and third time, it seemed altogether dull and ineffective." Then Lysias laughed, and said, "What then? Are you going to read it more than once to the jury?" And yet do but consider the persuasiveness and grace of

The drunken man prates only in his cups; but the talkative man prates everywhere.

Lysias' style; for he "I say was a great favourite with the dark-haired Muses." And of the things which have been said of Homer the truest is that he alone of all poets has survived the fastidiousness of mankind, as being ever new and still at his acme as regards giving pleasure, and yet saying and proclaiming about himself, "I hate to spin out a plain tale over and over again," he avoids and fears that satiety which lies in ambush for every narrative, and takes the hearer from one subject to another, and relieves by novelty the possibility of being surfeited. But the talkative worry one's ears to death with their tautologies, as people scribble the same things over and over again on palimpsests.

VI. Let us remind them then first of this, that just as in the case of wine, which was intended for pleasure and mirth, those who compel people to drink it neat and in large quantities bring some into a disgusting condition of drunkenness, so with speech, which is the pleasantest social tie amongst mankind, those who make a bad and ill-advised use of it render it unpleasing and unfit for company, paining those whom they think to gratify, and become a laughing-stock to those who they think admire them, and objectionable to those who they think love them. As then he cannot be a favourite of the goddess who with Aphrodite's charmed girdle repels and drives away those who associate with him, so he who with his speech bores and disgusts one is without either taste or refinement.

VII. Of all other passions and disorders some are dangerous, some hateful, some ridiculous, but in talkativeness all these elements are combined. For praters are jeered at for their commonplaces, and hated when they bring bad news, and run into danger when they reveal secrets. And so Anacharsis, when he was feasted by Solon and lay down to sleep, and was observed

The talkative worry one's ears to death with their tautologies, as people scribble the same things over and over again on palimpsests.

with his left hand on his private parts, and his right hand on his mouth, for he thought his tongue needed the stronger restraint, was right in his opinion. For it would be difficult to find as many men who have been ruined by venereal excesses as cities and leading states that have been undone by the utterance of a secret. When Sulla was besieging Athens, and had no time to waste there, "for he had other fish to fry," as Mithridates was ravaging Asia, and the party of Marius was again in power at Rome, some old men in a barber's shop happened to observe to one another that the Heptachalcon was not well guarded, and that their city ran a great risk of being captured at that point, and some spies who overheard this conversation reported it to Sulla. And he at once marched up his forces, and about midnight entered the city with his army, and all but rased it to the ground, and filled it with slaughter and dead bodies, insomuch that the Ceramicus ran with blood: and he was thus savage against the Athenians for their words rather than their deeds, for they had spoken ill of him and his wife Metella, jumping on to the walls and calling out in a jeering way,

"Sulla is a mulberry bestrewn with barley meal,"

and much similar banter. Thus they drew down upon themselves for words, which, as Plato says, are a very small matter, a very heavy punishment. The prating of one man also prevented Rome from becoming free by the removal of Nero. For it was only the night before the tyrant was to be murdered, and all preparations had been made, when he that was to do the deed going to the theatre, and seeing someone in chains near the doors who was about to be taken before Nero, and was bewailing his sad fortune, went up close to him and whispered, "Pray only, good sir, that to-day may pass by, to-morrow you will owe me many thanks."

A word once spoken cannot be recalled, but flies about and runs all round the world.

He guessing the meaning of the riddle, and thinking, I take it, "he is a fool who gives up what is in his hand for a remote contingency," preferred certain to honourable safety. For he informed Nero of what the man had said, and he was immediately arrested, and torture, and fire, and scourging were applied to him, who denied now in his necessity what before he had divulged without necessity.

VIII. Zeno the philosopher, that he might not against his will divulge any secrets when put to the torture, bit off his tongue, and spit it at the tyrant. Famous also was the reward which Leæna had for her taciturnity. She was the mistress of Harmodius and Aristogiton, and, although a woman, participated in their hopes of success in the conspiracy against the tyrants: for she had revelled in the glorious cup of love, and had been initiated in their secrets through the god. When then they had failed in their attempt and been put to death, and she was examined and bidden to reveal the names of the other conspirators, she refused to do so, and held out to the end, showing that those famous men in loving such a one as her had done nothing unworthy of them. And the Athenians erected to her memory a bronze lioness without a tongue, and placed it near the entrance to the Acropolis, signifying her dauntless courage by the nobleness of that animal, and by its being without a tongue her silence and fidelity. For no spoken word has done as much good as many unspoken ones. For at some future day we can give utterance if we like to what has been not said, but a word once spoken cannot be recalled, but flies about and runs all round the world. And this is the reason, I take it, why men teach us to speak, but the gods teach us to be silent, silence being enjoined on us in the mysteries and in all religious rites. Thus Homer has described the most eloquent Odysseus, and Telemachus, and Penelope, and the nurse, as all remarkable for their taciturnity. You remember the nurse saying,

Men teach us to speak, but the gods teach us to be silent.

"I'll keep it close as heart of oak or steel."

And Odysseus sitting by Penelope,

"Though in his heart he pitied her sad grief,
His eyes like horn or steel impassive stood
Within their lids, and craft his tears repressed."

So great control had he over all his body, and so much were all his members under the sway and rule of reason, that he commanded his eyes not to weep, his tongue not to speak, and his heart not to tremble or quake.

"So calm and passive did his heart remain,"

reason penetrating even to the irrational instincts, and making spirit and blood obedient and docile to it. Such also were most of his companions, for though they were dashed to the ground and dragged along by the Cyclops, they said not a word about Odysseus, nor did they show the stake of wood that had been put into the fire and prepared to put out Polyphemus' eye, but they would rather have been eaten alive than divulge secrets, such wonderful self-control and fidelity had they. And so it was not amiss of Pittacus, when the king of Egypt sent him a victim, and bade him take from it the best and worst piece of it, to pull out the tongue and send that to the king, as being the instrument of the greatest blessings and withal the greatest mischiefs.

IX. So Ino in Euripides, speaking plainly about herself, says she knows "how to be silent when she should, and to speak when speech is safe." For those who have enjoyed a truly noble and royal education learn first to be silent and then to speak. So the famous

Those who have enjoyed a truly noble and royal education learn first to be silent and then to speak.

It is better to be censured when one has done well by keeping one's counsel.

king Antigonus, when his son asked him, "When are we going to shift our quarters?" answered, "Are you afraid that you only will not hear the trumpet?" Was he afraid then to entrust a secret to him, to whom he intended one day to leave his kingdom? Nay rather, it was to teach him to be close and guarded on such matters. Metellus also, the well-known veteran, when questioned somewhat similarly about an expedition, said, "If I thought my coat knew the secret, I would strip it off and throw it into the fire." And Eumenes, when he heard that Craterus was marching against him, told none of his friends, but pretended that it was Neoptolemus; for his soldiers despised Neoptolemus, but they admired the glory and loved the virtue of Craterus; and no one but Eumenes knew the truth, and they engaged and were victorious, and unwittingly killed Craterus, and only recognized his dead body. So great a part did silence play in the battle, concealing the name of the enemy's general: so that Eumenes' friends marvelled more than found fault at his not having told them the truth. And if anyone should receive blame in such a case, it is better to be censured when one has done well by keeping one's counsel, rather than to have to accuse others through having come to grief by trusting them.

X. But, generally speaking, who has the right to blame the person who has not kept his secret? For if it was not to be known, it was not well to tell another person of it at all, and if you divulged your secret yourself and expected another person to keep it, you had more faith in another than in yourself. And so should he be such another as yourself you are deservedly undone, and should he be a better man than yourself, your safety is more than you could have reckoned on, as it involved finding a man more to be trusted than yourself. But you will say, He is my friend. Yes, but he has another friend, whom he reposes confidence in as much as you do in your friend, and that other friend has one of his own, and so on, so that the secret spreads in many quarters from inability to keep it close in one. For as the unit never deviates from its orbit, but (as its name signifies) always remains one, but the number two contains within it the seeds of infinity, for when it departs from itself it becomes plurality at once by doubling, so speech confined in one person's breast is truly secret, but if it be communicated to another it soon gets noised abroad. And so Homer calls words "winged," for as he that lets a bird go from his hands cannot easily get it back again, so he that lets a word go from his mouth cannot catch or stop it, but it is borne along "whirling on swift wings," and dispersed from one person to another. When a ship scuds before the gale the mariners can stop it, or at least check its course with cables and anchors, but when the spoken word once sails out of harbour, so to speak, there is no roadstead or anchorage for it, but borne along with much noise and echo it dashes its utterer on the rocks, and brings him into imminent danger of shipwreck,

> *"As one might set on fire Ida's woods*
> *With a small torch, so what one tells one person*
> *Is soon the property of all the citizens."*

XI. The Roman Senate had been discussing for several days a secret matter, and there was much doubt and suspicion about it. And one of the senators' wives, discreet in other matters but a very woman in curiosity, pressed her husband close, and entreated him to tell her what the secret was; she vowed and swore she would not divulge it, and did not refrain from shedding tears at her not being trusted. And he, nothing loth to convince her of her folly, said, "Your importunity, wife, has prevailed, listen to a dreadful and portentous matter. It has been told us by the priests

Homer calls words "winged," for as he that lets a bird go from his hands cannot easily get it back again, so he that lets a word go from his mouth cannot catch or stop it.

that a lark has been seen flying in the air with a golden helmet and spear: it is this portent that we are considering and discussing with the augurs, as to whether it be a good or bad omen. But say nothing about it." Having said these words he went into the Forum. But his wife seized on the very first of her maids that entered the room, and smote her breast, and tore her hair, and said, "Alas! for my husband and country! What will become of us?" wishing and teaching her maid to say, "Whatever's up?" So when she inquired she told her all about it, adding that refrain common to all praters, "Tell no one a word about it." The maid however had scarce left her mistress when she told one of her fellow-servants who was doing little or nothing, and she told her lover who happened to call at that moment. So the news spread to the Forum so quickly that it got the start of its original author, and one of his friends meeting him said, "Have you only just left your house?" "Only just," he replied. "Didn't you hear the news?" said his friend. "What news?" said he. "Why, that a lark has been seen flying in the air with a golden helmet and spear, and the Senate are met to discuss the portent." And he smiled and said to himself, "You are quick, wife, for the tale to get before me to the Forum!" Then meeting some of the Senators he disabused them of their panic. But to punish his wife, he said when he got home, "You have undone me, wife: for the secret has got abroad from my house, so that I must be an exile from my country for your inability to keep a secret." And on her trying to deny it, and saying, "Were there not three hundred Senators that heard of it as well as you? Might not one of them have divulged it?" he replied, "Stuff o' your three hundred! It was at your importunity that I invented the story, to put you to the test!" This fellow tested his wife warily and cunningly, as one pours water, and not wine or oil, into a leaky vessel.

When Fabius came into the Emperor's presence, and said, "Hail, Cæsar!" the Emperor replied, "Farewell, Fabius."

And Fabius, the friend of Augustus, hearing the Emperor in his old age mourning over the extinction of his family, how two of his daughter Julia's sons were dead, and how Posthumus Agrippa, the only remaining one, was in exile through false accusation, and how he was compelled to put his wife's son into the succession to the Empire, though he pitied Agrippa and had half a mind to recall him from banishment, repeated the Emperor's words to his wife, and she to Livia. And Livia bitterly upbraided Augustus, if he meant recalling his grandson, for not having done so long ago, instead of bringing her into hatred and hostility with the heir to the Empire. When Fabius came in the morning as usual into the Emperor's presence, and said, "Hail, Cæsar!" the Emperor replied, "Farewell, Fabius." And he understanding the meaning of this straightway went home, and sent for his wife, and said, "The Emperor knows that I have not kept his secret, so I shall kill myself." And his wife replied, "You have deserved your fate, since having been married to me so long you did not remember and guard against my incontinence of speech, but suffer me to kill myself first." So saying she took his sword, and slew herself first.

XII. That was a good answer therefore that the comic poet Philippides made to king Lysimachus, who greeted him kindly, and said to him, "What shall I give you of all my possessions?" "Whatever you like, O king, except your secrets." And talkativeness has another plague attached to it, even curiosity: for praters wish to hear much that they may have much to say, and most of all do they gad about to investigate and pry into secrets and hidden things, providing as it were an antiquated stock of rubbish for their twaddle, in fine like children who cannot hold ice in their hands, and yet are unwilling to let it go, or rather taking secrets to their bosoms and embracing them as if they were so many serpents, that they cannot control, but are sure to be

"What shall I give you of all my possessions?" "Whatever you like, O king, except your secrets."

27

gnawed to death by. They say that garfish and vipers burst in giving life to their young, so secrets by coming out ruin and destroy those who cannot keep them. Seleucus Callinicus having lost his army and all his forces in a battle against the Galati, threw off his diadem, and fled on a swift horse with an escort of three or four of his men a long day's journey by bypaths and out-of-the-way tracks, till faint and famishing for want of food he drew rein at a small farmhouse, where by chance he found the master at home, and asked for some bread and water. And he supplied him liberally and courteously not only with what he asked for but with whatever else was on the farm, and recognized the king, and being very joyful at this opportunity of ministering to the king's necessities, he could not contain himself, nor dissemble like the king who wished to be incognito, but he accompanied him to the road, and on parting from him, said, "Farewell, king Seleucus." And he stretching out his right hand, and drawing the man to him as if he was going to kiss him, gave a sign to one of his escorts to draw his sword and cut the man's head off;

"And at his word the head roll'd in the dust."

Whereas if he had been silent then, and kept his counsel for a time, as the king afterwards became prosperous and great, he would have received, I take it, greater favour for his silence than for his hospitality. And yet he had I admit some excuse for his want of reticence, namely hope and joy.

XIII. But most talkative people have no excuse for ruining themselves. As for example in a barber's shop one day there was some conversation about the tyranny of Dionysius, that it was as hard as adamant and invincible, and the barber laughed and said, "Fancy your saying this to me, who have my razor at his throat most

A talkative barber put the towel round his neck, and asked him, "How shall I shave you, O king?" "Silently," said the monarch.

days!" And Dionysius hearing this had him crucified. Barbers indeed are generally a talkative race, for people fond of prating flock to them and sit in their shops, so that they pick up the habit from their customers. It was a witty answer therefore of king Archelaus, when a talkative barber put the towel round his neck, and asked him, "How shall I shave you, O king?" "Silently," said the monarch. It was a barber that first spread the news of the great reverse of the Athenians in Sicily, having heard of it at the Piræus from a slave that had escaped from the island. He at once left his shop, and ran into the city at full speed, "that no one else should reap the fame, and he come in the second," of carrying the news into the town. And an uproar arising, as was only to be expected, the people assembled in the ecclesia, and began to investigate the origin of the rumour. So the barber was dragged up and questioned, but knew not the person's name who had told him, so was obliged to refer its origin to an anonymous and unknown person. Then anger filled the theatre, and the multitude cried out, "Torture the cursed fellow, put him to the rack: he has fabricated and concocted this news: who else heard it? who credits it?" The wheel was brought, the poor fellow stretched on it. Meantime those came up who had brought the news, who had escaped from the carnage in Sicily. Then all the multitude dispersed to weep over their private sorrows, and abandoned the poor barber, who remained fastened to the wheel. And when released late in the evening he actually asked the executioner, if they had heard how Nicias the General was slain. So invincible and incorrigible a vice does habit make talkativeness to be.

XIV. And yet, as those that drink bitter and strong-smelling physic are disgusted even with the cups they drink it out of, so those that bring evil tidings are disliked and hated by their hearers. Wittily therefore has Sophocles described the conversation between Creon and the guard.

Those that tell the tale grieve us as well as those that did the deed.

29

Terse and brief speakers, who put the maximum of matter into the minimum of words, are more admired and thought wiser than unbridled windbags.

"G. Is't in your ears or in your mind you're grieved?
C. Why do you thus define the seat of grief?
G. The doer pains your mind, but I your ears."

However those that tell the tale grieve us as well as those that did the deed: and yet there is no means of checking or controlling the running tongue. At Lacedæmon the temple of Athene Chalcioecus was broken into, and an empty flagon was observed lying on the ground inside, and a great concourse of people came up and discussed the matter. And one of the company said, "If you will allow me, I will tell you what I think about this flagon. I cannot help being of opinion that these sacrilegious wretches drank hemlock, and brought wine with them, before commencing their nefarious and dangerous work: that so, if they should fail to be detected, they might depart in safety, drinking the wine neat as an antidote to the hemlock: whereas should they be caught in the act, before they were put to the torture they would die of the poison easily and painlessly." When he had uttered these words, the idea seemed so ingenious and farfetched that it looked as if it could not emanate from fancy, but only from knowledge of the real facts. So the crowd surrounded this man, and asked him one after the other, "Who are you? Who knows you? How come you to know all this?" And at last he was convicted in this way, and confessed that he was one of those that had committed the sacrilege. And were not the murderers of Ibycus similarly captured? They were sitting in the theatre, and some cranes flew over their heads, and they laughed and whispered to one another, "Behold the avengers of Ibycus." And this being overheard by some who sat near, as Ibycus had now been some time missing and inquired after, they laid hold of this remark, and reported it to the magistrates. And so they were convicted and dragged off to punishment, being brought to justice not by the cranes but by their own inability to hold their tongues, being compelled by some Fury or Vengeance as it were to divulge the murder. For as in the body there is an attraction to sore and suffering parts from neighbouring parts, so the tongue of talkative persons, ever suffering from inflammation and a throbbing pulse, attracts and draws to it secret and hidden things. And so the tongue ought to be fenced in, and have reason ever before it, as a bulwark, to prevent its tripping: that we may not seem to be more silly than geese, of whom it is said that, when they fly from Cilicia over Mt. Taurus which swarms with eagles, they carry in their mouths a large stone, which they employ as a gag or bridle for their scream, and so they cross over by night unobserved.

XV. Now if anyone were to ask who is the worst and most abandoned man, no one would pass over the traitor, or mention anyone else. It was as the reward of treason that Euthycrates roofed his house with Macedonian wood, as Demosthenes tells us; and that Philocrates got a large sum of money, and spent it on women and fish; and it was for betraying Eretria that Euphorbus and Philagrus got an estate from king Philip. But the talkative man is an unhired and officious traitor, not of horses or walls, but of secrets which he divulges in the law courts, in factions, in party-strife, no one thanking him for his pains; but should anyone listen to him he thinks he is the obliged party. So that what was said to a man who rashly and indiscriminately squandered away all his means and bestowed them on others,

> "It is not kindness in you but disease,
> This itch for giving,"

is appropriate also to the prater, "You don't communicate to us all this out of friendship or goodwill, but it is a disease in you, this itch for talking and prating."

When Philip wrote to them, "If I invade Laconia, I will drive you all out of house and home," they only wrote back, "If."

XVI. But all this must not be looked upon merely as an indictment against talkativeness, but an attempt to cure it: for we overcome the passions by judgement and practice, but judgement is the first step. For no one is wont to shun, and eradicate from his soul, what he does not dislike. And we dislike the passions only when we discern by reason the harm and shame that results to us by indulging them. As we see every day in the case of talkative people: if they wish to be loved, they are hated; if they desire to please, they bore; when they think they are admired, they are really laughed at; they spend, and get no gain from so doing; they injure their friends, benefit their enemies, and ruin themselves. So that the first cure and remedy of this disorder will be to reckon up the shame and trouble that results from it.

XVII. In the next place we must consider the opposite virtue to talkativeness, always listening to and having on our lips the encomiums passed upon reserve, and remembering the decorum sanctity and mysterious power of silence, and ever bearing in mind that terse and brief speakers, who put the maximum of matter into the minimum of words, are more admired and esteemed and thought wiser than unbridled windbags. And so Plato praises, and compares to clever javelin-men, such as speak tersely, compressedly, and concisely. And Lycurgus by using his citizens from boyhood to silence taught them to perfection their brevity and terseness. For as the Celtiberians make steel of iron only after digging down deep in the soil, and carefully separating the iron ore, so Laconian oratory has no rind, but by the removal of all superfluous matter goes home straight to the point like steel. For its sententiousness, and pointed suppleness in repartee, comes from the habit of silence. And we ought to quote such pointed sayings especially to talkative people, such neatness and vigour have they, as, for example, what the

Harmony would make them strong and hard to overthrow, while dissension would make them feeble.

Lacedæmonians said to Philip, "[Remember] Dionysius at Corinth." And again, when Philip wrote to them, "If I invade Laconia, I will drive you all out of house and home," they only wrote back, "If." And when king Demetrius was indignant and cried out, "The Lacedæmonians have only sent me one ambassador," the ambassador was not frightened but said, "Yes, one to one man." Certainly among the ancients men of few words were admired. So the Amphictyones did not write extracts from the Iliad or Odyssey, or the Pæans of Pindar, in the temple of Pythian Apollo at Delphi, but "Know thyself," "Not too much of anything," and "Be a surety, trouble is near;" so much did they admire compactness and simplicity of speech, combining brevity with shrewdness of mind. And is not the god himself short and concise in his oracles? Is he not called Loxias, because he prefers ambiguity to longwindedness? And are not those who express their meaning by signs without words wonderfully praised and admired? As Heraclitus, when some of the citizens asked him to give them his opinion about concord, got on the platform, and took a cup of cold water, and put some barley-meal in it, and stirred it up with penny-royal, thus showing them that it is being content with anything, and not needing costly dainties, that keeps cities in peace and concord. Scilurus, the king of the Scythians, left eighty sons, and on his death-bed asked for a bundle of sticks, and bade his sons break it when it was tied together, and when they could not, he took the sticks one by one and easily broke them all up: thus showing them that their harmony and concord would make them strong and hard to overthrow, while dissension would make them feeble and insecure.

XVIII. If then anyone were continually to recollect and repeat these or similar terse sayings, he would probably cease to be

It is not by applying bit or bridle that we can restrain the talkative person, we must master the disease by habit.

pleased with idle talk. As for myself, when I consider of what importance it is to attend to reason, and to keep to one's purpose, I confess I am quite put out of countenance by the example of the slave of Pupius Piso the orator. He, not wishing to be annoyed by their prating, ordered his slaves merely to answer his questions, and not say a word more. On one occasion wishing to pay honour to Clodius who was then in power, he ordered him to be invited to his house, and provided for him no doubt a sumptuous entertainment. At the time fixed all the guests were present except Clodius, for whom they waited, and the host frequently sent the slave who used to invite guests to see if he was coming, but when evening came, and he was now quite despaired of, he said to his slave, "Did you not invite him?" "Certainly," said the slave. "Why then has he not come?" said the master. "Because he declined," said the slave. "Why then did you not tell me of it at once?" said the master. "Because you never asked me," said the slave. This was a Roman slave. But an Athenian slave "while digging will tell his master on what terms peace was made." So great is the force of habit in all matters. And of it we will now speak.

He who without being asked undertakes to answer a question is disagreeable even if he succeeds.

XIX. For it is not by applying bit or bridle that we can restrain the talkative person, we must master the disease by habit. In the first place then, when you are in company and questions are going round, accustom yourself not to speak till all the rest have declined giving an answer. For as Sophocles says, "counsel is not like a race;" no more are question and answer. For in a race the victory belongs to him who gets in first, but in company, if anyone has given a satisfactory answer, it is sufficient by assenting and agreeing to his view to get the reputation of being a pleasant fellow; and if no satisfactory answer is given, then to enlighten ignorance and supply the necessary information is well-timed and does not excite envy. But let us be especially on our guard that, if anyone else is asked a question, we do not ourselves anticipate and intercept him in giving an answer. It is indeed perhaps nowhere good form, if another is asked a favour, to push him aside and undertake to grant it ourselves; for we shall seem so to upbraid two people at once, the one who was asked as not able to grant the favour, and the other as not knowing how to ask in the right quarter. But especially insulting is such forwardness and impetuosity in answering questions. For he that anticipates by his own answer the person that was asked the question seems to say, "What is the good of asking him? What does he know about it? In my presence nobody else ought to be asked about these matters." And yet we often put questions to people, not so much because we want an answer, as to elicit from them conversation and friendly feeling, and from a wish to fit them for company, as Socrates drew out Theætetus and Charmides. For it is all one to run up and kiss one who wishes to be kissed by another, or to divert to oneself the attention that he was bestowing on another, as to intercept another person's answers, and to transfer people's ears, and force their attention, and fix them on oneself; when, even if he that was asked declines to give an answer, it will be well to hold oneself in reserve, and only to meet the question modestly when one's turn comes, so framing one's answer as to seem to oblige the person who asked the question, and as if one had been appealed to for an answer by the other. For if people are asked questions and cannot give a satisfactory answer they are with justice excused; but he who without being asked undertakes to answer a question, and anticipates another, is disagreeable even if he succeeds, while, if his answer is unsatisfactory, he is ridiculed by all the company, and his failure is a source of the liveliest satisfaction to them.

There are three kinds of answers to questions, the necessary, the polite, and the superfluous.

*Delight has a
voice of its own,
and leads about
the tongue in
its train, ever
wishing to fortify
it with memory.*

XX. The next thing to practise oneself to in answering the
questions put to one,—a point to which the talkative person ought
to pay the greatest attention,—is not through inadvertence to give
serious answers to people who only challenge you to talk in fun
and sport. For some people concoct questions not for real
information, but simply for amusement and to pass the time away,
and propound them to talkative people, just to have them on.
Against this we must be on our guard, and not rush into
conversation too hastily, or as if we were obliged for the chance,
but we must consider the character of the inquirer and his
purpose. When it seems that he really desires information, we
should accustom ourselves to pause, and interpose some interval
between the question and answer; during which time the
questioner can add anything if he chooses, and the other can
reflect on his answer, and not be in too great a hurry about it, nor
bury it in obscurity, nor, as is frequently the case in too great
haste, answer some other question than that which was asked. The
Pythian Priestess indeed was accustomed to utter some of her
oracles at the very moment before the question was put: for the
god whom she serves "understands the dumb, and hears the
mute." But he that wishes to give an appropriate answer must
carefully consider both the question and the mind of the
questioner, lest it be as the proverb expresses it,

"I asked for shovels, they denied me pails."

Besides we ought to check this greediness and hunger for words,
that it may not seem as if we had a flood on our tongue which was
dammed up, but which we were only too glad to discharge on a
question being put. Socrates indeed so repressed his thirst, that
he would not allow himself to drink after exercise in the
gymnasium, till he had first drawn from the well one bucket of

water and poured it on to the ground, that he might accustom his irrational part to wait upon reason.

XXI. There are moreover three kinds of answers to questions, the necessary, the polite, and the superfluous. For instance, if anyone asked, "Is Socrates at home?" one, as if backward and disinclined to answer, might say, "Not at home;" or, if he wished to speak with Laconic brevity, might cut off "at home," and simply say "No;" as, when Philip wrote to the Lacedæmonians to ask if they would receive him in their city, they sent him back merely a large "No." But another would answer more politely, "He is not at home, but with the bankers," and if he wished to add a little more, "he expects to see some strangers there." But the superfluous prater, if he has read Antimachus of Colophon, says, "He is not at home, but with the bankers, waiting for some Ionian strangers, about whom he has had a letter from Alcibiades who is in the neighbourhood of Miletus, staying with Tissaphernes the satrap of the great king, who used long ago to favour the Lacedæmonian party, but now attaches himself to the Athenians for Alcibiades' sake, for Alcibiades desires to return to his country, and so has succeeded in changing the views of Tissaphernes." And then he will go over the whole of the Eighth Book of Thucydides, and deluge the man, till before he is aware Miletus is captured, and Alcibiades is in exile the second time. In such a case most of all ought we to curtail talkativeness, by following the track of a question closely, and tracing out our answer according to the need of the questioner with the same accuracy as we describe a circle. When Carneades was disputing in the gymnasium before the days of his great fame, the superintendent of the gymnasium sent to him a message to bid him modulate his voice (for it was of the loudest), and when he asked him to fix a standard, the superintendent replied not amiss, "The standard of the person

Prating is less of a nuisance when it is on some literary subject.

talking with you." So the meaning of the questioner ought to be the standard for the answer.

XXII. Moreover as Socrates urged his disciples to abstain from such food as tempted them to eat when they were not hungry, and from such drinks as tempted them to drink when they were not thirsty, so the talkative person ought to be afraid most of such subjects of conversation as he most delights in and repeats *ad nauseam*, and to try and resist their influence. For example, soldiers are fond of descriptions about war, and thus Homer introduces Nestor frequently narrating his prowess and glorious deeds. And generally speaking those who have been successful in the law courts, or beyond their hopes been favourites of kings and princes, are possessed, as it were by some disease, with the itch for frequently recalling and narrating, how they got on and were advanced, what struggles they underwent, how they argued on some famous occasion, how they won the day either as plaintiffs or defendants, what panegyrics were showered upon them. For joy is much more inclined to prate than the well-known sleeplessness represented in comedies, frequently rousing itself, and finding something fresh to relate. And so at any excuse they slip into such narratives. For not only,

"Where anyone does itch, there goes his hand,"

What is this word that is so eager for utterance?

but also delight has a voice of its own, and leads about the tongue in its train, ever wishing to fortify it with memory. Thus lovers spend most of their time in conversations that revive the memory of their loves; and if they cannot talk to human beings about them, they talk about them to inanimate objects, as, "O dearest bed," and,

On Contentedness of Mind

*"O happy lamp, Bacchis deems you a god,
And if she thinks so, then you are indeed
The greatest of the gods."*

*Words may be
idle and useless
as well as deeds.*

The talkative person therefore is merely as regards words a white line, but he that is especially inclined to certain subjects should be especially on his guard against talking about them, and should avoid such topics, since from the pleasure they give him they may entice him to be very prolix and tedious. The same is the case with people in regard to such subjects as they think they are more experienced in and acquainted with than others. For such a one, being self-appreciative and fond of fame, "spends most of the day in that particular branch of study in which he chances to be proficient." Thus he that is fond of reading will give his time to research; the grammarian his to syntax; and the traveller, who has wandered over many countries, his to geography. We must therefore be on our guard against our favourite topics, for they are an enticement to talkativeness, as its wonted haunts are to an animal. Admirable therefore was the behaviour of Cyrus in challenging his companions, not to those contests in which he was superior to them, but to those in which he was inferior, partly that he might not give them pain through his superiority, partly for his own benefit by learning from them. But the talkative person acts just contrary, for if any subject is introduced from which he might learn something he did not know, this he rejects and refuses, not being able to earn a good deal by a short silence, but he rambles round the subject and babbles out stale and commonplace rhapsodies. As one amongst us, who by chance had read two or three of the books of Ephorus, bored everybody, and dispersed every social party, by always narrating the particulars of the battle of Leuctra and its consequences, so that he got nicknamed Epaminondas.

XXIII. Nevertheless this is one of the least of the evils of talkativeness, and we ought even to try and divert it into such channels as these, for prating is less of a nuisance when it is on some literary subject. We ought also to try and get some persons to write on some topic, and so discuss it by themselves. For Antipater the Stoic philosopher, not being able or willing it seems to dispute with Carneades, who inveighed vehemently against the Stoic philosophy, writing and filling many books of controversy against him, got the nickname of *Noisy-with-the-pen*; and perhaps the exercise and excitement of writing, keeping him very much apart from the community, might make the talkative man by degrees better company to those he associated with; as dogs, bestowing their rage on sticks and stones, are less savage to men. It will also be very advantageous for such to mix with people better and older than themselves, for they will accustom themselves to be silent by standing in awe of their reputation. And withal it will be well, when we are going to say something, and the words are on our lips, to reflect and consider, "What is this word that is so eager for utterance? To what is this tongue marching? What good will come of speaking now, or what harm of silence?" For we ought not to drop words as we should a burden that pressed upon us, for the word remains still after it has been spoken just the same; but men speak either on their own behalf if they want something, or to benefit those that hear them, or, to gratify one another, they season everyday life with speech, as one seasons food with salt. But if words are neither useful to the speaker, nor necessary for the hearer, nor contain any pleasure or charm, why are they spoken? For words may be idle and useless as well as deeds. And besides all this we must ever remember as most important the dictum of Simonides, that he had often repented he had spoken, but never that he had been silent: while as to the power and strength of practice consider how men by

Silence is never thirsty, as Hippocrates says.

much toil and painstaking will get rid even of a cough or hiccough. And silence is not only never thirsty, as Hippocrates says, but also never brings pain or sorrow.

On Curiosity.

I f a house is dark, or has little air, is in an exposed position, or unhealthy, the best thing will probably be to leave it; but if one is attached to it from long residence in it, one can improve it and make it more light and airy and healthy by altering the position of the windows and stairs, and by throwing open new doors and shutting up old ones. So some towns have been altered for the better, as my native place, which did lie to the west and received the rays of the setting sun from Parnassus, was they say turned to the east by Chæron. And Empedocles the naturalist is supposed to have driven away the pestilence from that district, by having closed up a mountain gorge that was prejudicial to health by admitting the south wind to the plains. Similarly, as there are certain diseases of the soul that are injurious and harmful and bring storm and darkness to it, the best thing will be to eject them and lay them low by giving them open sky, pure air and light, or, if that cannot be, to change and improve them some way or other. One such mental disease, that immediately suggests itself to one, is curiosity, the desire to know other people's troubles, a disease that seems neither free from envy nor malignity.

> *"Malignant wretch, why art so keen to mark*
> *Thy neighbour's fault, and seest not thine own?"*

Shift your view, and turn your curiosity so as to look inwards: if you delight to study the history of evils, you have copious material at home, "as much as there is water in the Alizon, or leaves on the oak," such a quantity of faults will you find in your own life, and passions in your soul, and shortcomings in your duty. For as Xenophon says good managers have one place for the vessels they use in sacrificing, and another for those they use at meals, one place for their farm instruments, and another for their weapons of war, so your faults arise from different causes, some from envy, some from jealousy, some from cowardice, some from meanness. Review these, consider these; bar up the curiosity that pries into your neighbours' windows and passages, and open it on the men's apartments, and women's apartments, and servant's attics, in your own house. There this inquisitiveness and curiosity will find full vent, in inquiries that will not be useless or malicious, but advantageous and serviceable, each one saying to himself,

"What have I done amiss? What have I done?
What that I ought to have done left undone?"

Turn your curiosity so as to look inwards: if you delight to study the history of evils, you have copious material at home.

II. And now, as they say of Lamia that she is blind when she sleeps at home, for she puts her eyes on her dressing-table, but when she goes out she puts her eyes on again, and has good sight, so each of us turns, like an eye, our malicious curiosity out of doors and on others, while we are frequently blind and ignorant about our own faults and vices, not applying to them our eyes and light. So that the curious man is more use to his enemies than to himself, for he finds fault with and exposes their shortcomings, and shows them what they ought to avoid and correct, while he neglects most of his affairs at home, owing to his excitement about things abroad. Odysseus indeed would not converse with his mother till he had learnt from the seer Tiresias what he went to Hades to learn; and after receiving that information, then he turned to her, and asked questions about the other women, who Tyro was, and who the fair Chloris, and why Epicaste had died, "having fastened a noose with a long drop to the lofty beam." But we, while very remiss and ignorant and careless about ourselves, know all about the pedigrees of other people, that our neighbour's grandfather was a Syrian, and his grandmother a Thracian woman, and that such a one owes three talents, and has not paid the interest. We even inquire into such trifling matters as where somebody's wife has been, and what those two are talking in the corner about. But Socrates used to busy himself in examining the secret of Pythagoras' persuasive oratory, and Aristippus, meeting Ischomachus at the Olympian games, asked him how Socrates conversed so as to have so much influence over the young men, and having received from him a few scraps and samples of his style, was so enthusiastic about it that he wasted away, and became quite pale and lean, thirsty and parched, till he sailed to Athens and drew from the fountain-head, and knew the wonderful man himself and his speeches and philosophy, the object of which was that men should recognize their faults and so get rid of them.

III. But some men cannot bear to look upon their own life, so unlovely a spectacle is it, nor to throw and flash on themselves, like a lantern, the reflection of reason; but their soul being burdened with all manner of vices, and dreading and shuddering at its own interior, sallies forth and wanders abroad, feeding and fattening its malignity there. For as a hen, when its food stands near its coop, will frequently slip off into a corner and scratch up,

"Where I ween some poor little grain appears on the dunghill,"

The curious man is more use to his enemies than to himself, for he exposes their shortcomings, and shows them what they ought to avoid and correct.

so curious people neglecting conversation or inquiry about common matters, such as no one would try and prevent or be indignant at their prying into, pick out the secret and hidden troubles of every family. And yet that was a witty answer of the Egyptian, to the person who asked him, "What he was carrying wrapped up;" "It was wrapped up on purpose that you should not know." And you too, Sir, I would say to a curious person, why do you pry into what is hidden? If it were not something bad it would not be hidden. Indeed it is not usual to go into a strange house without knocking at the door, and nowadays there are porters, but in old times there were knockers on doors to let the people inside know when anyone called, that a stranger might not find the mistress or daughter of the house *en déshabille*, or one of the slaves being corrected, or the maids bawling out. But the curious person intrudes on all such occasions as these, although he would be unwilling to be a spectator, even if invited, of a well-ordered family: but the things for which bars and bolts and doors are required, these he reveals and divulges openly to others. Those are the most troublesome winds, as Aristo says, that blow up our clothes: but the curious person not only strips off the garments and clothes of his neighbours, but breaks through their walls, opens their doors, and like the wanton wind, that insinuates itself into maidenly reserve, he pries into and calumniates dances and routs and revels.

Those that pry into the troubles of great people ruin themselves before they get the knowledge they desire.

IV. And as Cleon is satirized in the play as having "his hands among the Ætolians, but his soul in Peculation-town," so the soul of the curious man is at once in the mansions of the rich, and the cottages of the poor, and the courts of kings, and the bridal chambers of the newly married; he pries into everything, the affairs of foreigners, the affairs of princes, and sometimes not without danger. For just as if one were to taste aconite to investigate its properties, and kill oneself before one had discovered them, so those that pry into the troubles of great people ruin themselves before they get the knowledge they desire; even as those become blind who, neglecting the wide and general diffusion all over the earth of the sun's rays, impudently attempt to gaze at its orb and penetrate to its light. And so that was a wise answer of Philippides the Comic Poet, when King Lysimachus asked him on one occasion, "What would you like to have of mine?" "Anything, O king, but your secrets." For the pleasantest and finest things to be got from kings are public, as banquets, and riches, and festivities, and favours: but come not near any secret of theirs, pry not into it. There is no concealment of the joy of a prosperous monarch, or of his laugh when he is in a playful mood, or of any tokens of his goodwill and favour; but dreadful is what he conceals, his gloominess, his sternness, his reserve, his store of latent wrath, his meditation on stern revenge, his jealousy of his wife, or suspicion of his son, or doubt about the fidelity of a friend. Flee from this cloud that is so black and threatening, for when its hidden fury bursts forth, you will not fail to hear its thunder and see its lightning.

V. How shall you flee from it? Why, by dissipating and distracting your curiosity, by turning your soul to better and pleasanter objects: examine the phenomena of sky, and earth, and air, and sea. Are you by nature fond of gazing at little or great things? If at great, turn your attention to the sun, consider its rising and setting: view the changes of the moon, like the changes of our mortal life, see how it waxes and wanes,

> *"How at the first it peers out small and dim*
> *Till it unfolds its full and glorious Orb,*

View the changes of the moon, like the changes of our mortal life, see how it waxes and wanes.

47

If you must ever bestow your time and attention on what is bad, go to history, and turn your eye on the sum total of human misery.

And when its zenith it has once attained,
Again it wanes, grows small, and disappears."

These are indeed Nature's secrets, but they bring no trouble on those that study them. But if you decline the study of great things, inspect with curiosity smaller matters, see how some plants flourish, are green and gay, and exhibit their beauty, all the year round, while others are sometimes gay like them, at other times, like some unthrift, run through their resources entirely, and are left bare and naked. Consider again their various shapes, how some produce oblong fruits, others angular, others smooth and round. But perhaps you will not care to pry into all this, since you will find nothing bad. If you must then ever bestow your time and attention on what is bad, as the serpent lives but in deadly matter, go to history, and turn your eye on the sum total of human misery. For there you will find "the falls of men, and murders of their lives," rapes of women, attacks of slaves, treachery of friends, mixing of poisons, envyings, jealousies, "shipwrecks of families," and dethroning of princes. Sate and cloy yourself on these, you will by so doing vex and enrage none of your associates.

VI. But it seems curiosity does not rejoice in stale evils, but only in fresh and recent ones, gladly viewing the spectacle of tragedies of yesterday, but backward in taking part in comic and festive scenes. And so the curious person is a languid and listless hearer to the narrator of a marriage, or sacrifice, or solemn procession, he says he has heard most of all that before, bids the narrator cut it short and come to the point; but if his visitor tell him of the violation of some girl, or the adultery of some married woman, or the disputes and intended litigation of brothers, he doesn't go to sleep then, nor pretend want of leisure,

"But he pricks up his ears, and asks for more."

And indeed those lines,

"Alas! how quicker far to mortals' ears
Do ill news travel than the news of good!"

are truly said of curious people. For as cupping-glasses take away the worst blood, so the ears of curious people attract only the worst reports; or rather, as cities have certain ominous and gloomy gates, through which they conduct only condemned criminals, or convey filth and night soil, for nothing pure or holy has either ingress into or egress from them, so into the ears of curious people goes nothing good or elegant, but tales of murders travel and lodge there, wafting a whiff of unholy and obscene narrations.

"And ever in my house is heard alone
The sound of wailing;"

this is to the curious their one Muse and Siren, this the sweetest note they can hear. For curiosity desires to know what is hidden and secret; but no one conceals his good fortune, nay sometimes people even pretend to have such advantages as they do not really possess. So the curious man, eager to hear a history of what is bad, is possessed by the passion of malignity, which is brother to envy and jealousy. For envy is pain at another's blessings, and malignity is joy at another's misfortunes: and both proceed from the same savage and brutish vice, ill-nature.

VII. But so unpleasant is it to everybody to have his private ills brought to light, that many have died rather than acquaint the doctors with their secret ailments. For suppose Herophilus, or

Envy is pain at another's blessings, and malignity is joy at another's misfortunes: and both proceed from the same vice, ill-nature.

Erasistratus, or even Æsculapius himself during his sojourn on earth, had gone with their drugs and surgical instruments from house to house, to inquire what man had a fistula in ano, or what woman had a cancer in her womb;—and yet their curiosity would have been professional—who would not have driven them away from their house, for not waiting till they were sent for, and for coming without being asked to spy out their neighbours' ailments? But curious people pry into these and even worse matters, not from a desire to heal them, but only to expose them to others, which makes them deservedly hated. For we are not vexed and mortified with custom-house officers when they levy toll on goods *bona fide* imported, but only when they seek for contraband articles, and rip up bags and packages: and yet the law allows them to do even this, and sometimes it is injurious to them not to do so. But curious people abandon and neglect their own affairs, and are busy about their neighbours' concerns. Seldom do they go into the country, for they do not care for its quiet and stillness and solitude, but if once in a way they do go there, they look more at their neighbours' vines than their own, and inquire how many cows of their neighbour have died, or how much of his wine has turned sour, and when they are satisfied on these points they soon return to town again. But the genuine countryman does not willingly listen to any rumour that chances to come from the town, for he quotes the following lines,

> *"Even with spade in hand he'll tell the terms*
> *On which peace was concluded: all these things*
> *The cursèd fellow walks about and pries into."*

VIII. But curious people shun the country as stale and dull and too quiet, and push into warehouses and markets and harbours, asking, "Any news? Were you not in the market in the forenoon?"

As cooks pray for plenty of meat, and fishmongers for shoals of fish, so curious people pray for shoals of trouble.

and sometimes receiving for answer, "What then? Do you think things in the town change every three hours?" Notwithstanding if anyone brings any news, he'll get off his horse, and embrace him, and kiss him, and stand to listen. If however the person who meets him says he has no news, he will say somewhat peevishly, "No news, Sir? Have you not been in the market? Did you not pass by the officers' quarters? Did you exchange no words with those that have just arrived from Italy?" To stop such people the Locrian authorities had an excellent rule; they fined everyone coming from abroad who asked what the news was. For as cooks pray for plenty of meat, and fishmongers for shoals of fish, so curious people pray for shoals of trouble, and plenty of business, and innovations and changes, that they may have something to hunt after and tittle-tattle about. Well also was it in *Charondas*, the legislator of the people of Thurii, to forbid any of the citizens but adulterers and curious persons to be ridiculed on the stage. Adultery itself indeed seems to be only the fruit of curiosity about another man's pleasures, and an inquiring and prying into things kept close and hidden from the world; while curiosity is a tampering with and seduction of and revealing the nakedness of secrets.

IX. As it is likely that much learning will produce wordiness, and so Pythagoras enjoined five years' silence on his scholars, calling it a truce from words, so defamation of character is sure to go with curiosity. For what people are glad to hear they are glad to talk about, and what they eagerly pick up from others they joyfully retail to others. And so, amongst the other mischiefs of curiosity, the disease runs counter to their desires; for all people fight shy of them, and conceal their affairs from them, and neither care to do or say anything in their presence, but defer consultations, and put off investigations, till such people are out

It is likely that much learning will produce wordiness, and so Pythagoras enjoined five years' silence on his scholars, calling it a truce from words.

of the way; and if, when some secret is just about to be uttered, or some important business is just about to be arranged, some curious man happen to pop in, they are mum at once and reserved, as one puts away fish if the cat is about; and so frequently things seen and talked about by all the rest of the world are unknown only to them. For the same reason the curious person never gets the confidence of anybody. For we would rather entrust our letters and papers and seals to slaves and strangers than to curious friends and intimates. The famous Bellerophon, though he carried letters against his life, opened them not, but abstained from reading the letter to the king, as he had refused to sell his honour to Proetus' wife, so great was his continence. For curiosity and adultery both come from incontinence, and to the latter is added monstrous folly and insanity. For to pass by so many common and public women, and to intrude oneself on some married woman, who is sure to be more costly, and possibly less pretty to boot, is the acme of madness. Yet such is the conduct of curious people. They neglect many gay sights, fail to hear much that would be well worth hearing, lose much fine sport and pastime, to break open private letters, to put their ears to their neighbour's walls, and to whisper to their slaves and women-servants, practices always low, and frequently dangerous.

The piling up of other people's misdoings is indecent and useless.

X. It will be exceedingly useful, therefore, to deter the curious from these propensities, for them to remember their past experience. Simonides used to say that he occasionally opened two chests for rewards and thanks that he had by him, and found the one full for rewards, but the one for thanks always empty. So if anyone were to open occasionally the stores that curiosity had amassed, and observe what a cargo there was of useless and idle and unlovely things, perhaps the sight of all this poor stuff would inspire him with disgust. Suppose someone, in studying the writings of the ancients, were to pick out only their worst passages, and compile them into a volume, as Homer's imperfect lines, and the solecisms of the tragedians, and Archilochus' indecent and bitter railings against women, by which he so exposed himself, would he not be worthy of the curse of the tragedian,

"Perish, compiler of thy neighbours' ills?"

And independently of such a curse, the piling up of other people's misdoings is indecent and useless, and like the town which Philip founded and filled with the vilest and most dissolute wretches, and called *Rogue Town*. Curious persons, indeed, making a collection of the faults and errors and solecisms, not of lines or poems but of people's lives, render their memory a most inelegant and unlovely register of dark deeds. Just as there are in Rome some people who care nothing for pictures and statues, or even handsome boys or women exposed for sale, but haunt the monster-market, and make eager inquiries about people who have no calves, or three eyes, or arms like weasels, or heads like ostriches, and look about for some

"Unnatural monster like the Minotaur,"

and for a time are greatly captivated with them, but if anyone continually gazes at such sights, they will soon give him satiety and disgust; so let those who curiously inquire into the errors and faults of life, and disgraces of families, and disorders in other people's houses, first remember what little favour or advantage such prying has brought them on previous occasions.

XI. Habit will be of the utmost importance in stopping this propensity, if we begin early to practise self-control in respect to it,

It is all one whether one puts one's feet or eyes in another person's house.

The senses ought not to rove about when sent on an errand by the soul.

for as the disease increases by habit and degrees, so will its cure, as we shall see when we discuss the necessary discipline. In the first place, let us begin with the most trifling and unimportant matters. What hardship will it be when we walk abroad not to read the epitaphs on graves, or what detriment shall we suffer by not glancing at the inscriptions on walls in the public walks? Let us reflect that there is nothing useful or pleasant for us in these notices, which only record that so-and-so remembered so-and-so out of gratitude, and, "Here lies the best of friends," and much poor stuff of that kind; which indeed do not seem to do much harm, except indirectly, to those that read them, by engendering the practice of curiosity about things immaterial. And as huntsmen do not allow the hounds to follow any scent and run where they please, but check and restrain them in leashes, keeping their sense of smell pure and fresh for the object of their chase, that they may the keener dart on their tracks, "following up the traces of the unfortunate beasts by their scent," so we must check and repress the sallies and excursions of the curious man to every object of interest, whether of sight or hearing, and confine him to what is useful. For as eagles and lions on the prowl keep their claws sheathed that they may not lose their edge and sharpness, so, when we remember that curiosity for learning has also its edge and keenness, let us not entirely expend or blunt it on inferior objects.

XII. Next let us accustom ourselves when we pass a strange house not to look inside at the door, or curiously inspect the interior, as if we were going to pilfer something, remembering always that saying of Xenocrates, that it is all one whether one puts one's feet or eyes in another person's house. For such prying is neither honourable, nor comely, nor even agreeable.

"Stranger, thou'lt see within untoward sights."

On Contentedness of Mind

For such is generally the condition inside houses, utensils kicking about, maids lolling about, no work going on, nothing to please the eye; and moreover such side glances, and stray shots as it were, distort the soul, and are unhandsome, and the practice is a pernicious one. When Diogenes saw Dioxippus, a victor at Olympia, driving up in his chariot and unable to take his eyes off a handsome woman who was watching the procession, but still turning round and casting sheep's eyes at her, he said, "See you yon athlete straining his neck to look at a girl?" And similarly you may see curious people twisting and straining their necks at every spectacle alike, from the habit and practice of turning their eyes in all directions. And I think the senses ought not to rove about, like an ill-trained maid, when sent on an errand by the soul, but to do their business, and then return quickly with the answer, and afterwards to keep within the bounds of reason, and obey her behests. But it is like those lines of Sophocles,

> *"Then did the Ænianian's horses bolt,*
> *Unmanageable quite;"*

for so the senses not having, as we said, right training and practice, often run away, and drag reason along with them, and plunge her into unlawful excesses. And so, though that story about Democritus is false, that he purposely destroyed his eyesight by the reflection from burning-glasses (as people sometimes shut up windows that look into the street), that they might not disturb him by frequently calling off his attention to external things, but allow him to confine himself to purely intellectual matters, yet it is very true in every case that those who use the mind most are least acted upon by the senses. And so the philosophers erected their places for study as far as possible from towns, and called Night the time propitious to thought, thinking

The philosophers erected their places for study as far as possible from towns, and called Night the time propitious to thought.

quiet and withdrawal from worldly distractions a great help towards meditating upon and solving the problems of life.

XIII. Moreover, when men are abusing and reviling one another in the market-place, it is not very difficult or tiresome not to go near them; or if a tumultuous concourse of people crowd together, to remain seated; or to get up and go away, if you are not master of yourself. For you will gain no advantage by mixing yourself up with curious people: but you will derive the greatest benefit from putting a force upon your inclinations, and bridling your curiosity, and accustoming it to obey reason. Afterwards it will be well to extend the practice still further, and not to go to the theatre when some fine piece is performing, and if your friends invite you to see some dancer or actor to decline, and, if there is some shouting in the stadium and hippodrome, not even to turn your head to look what is up. For as Socrates advised people to abstain from food that made them eat when they were not hungry, and from drinks that made them drink when they were not thirsty, so ought we also to shun and flee from those objects of interest, whether to eye or ear, that master us and attract us when we stand in no need of them. Thus Cyrus would not look at Panthea, but when Araspes told him that her beauty was well worth inspection, he replied, "For that very reason must I the more abstain from seeing her, for if at your persuasion I were to pay her a visit, perhaps she would persuade me to visit her again when I could ill spare the time, so that I might neglect important business to sit with her and gaze on her charms." Similarly Alexander would not see the wife of Darius, who was reputed to be very beautiful, but visited her mother who was old, and would not venture to look upon the young and handsome queen. We on the contrary peep into women's litters, and hang about their windows, and think we do no harm, though we thus make our curiosity a loop-hole for all manner of vice.

Flee from those objects of interest, whether to eye or ear, that master us and attract us when we stand in no need of them.

XIV. Moreover, as it is of great help to fair dealing sometimes not to seize some honest gain, that you may accustom yourself as far as possible to flee from unjust gains, and as it makes greatly for virtue to abstain sometimes from your own wife, that you may not ever be tempted by another woman, so, applying the habit to curiosity, try not to see and hear at times all that goes on in your own house even, and if anyone wishes to tell you anything about it give him the go-by, and decline to hear him. For it was nothing but his curiosity that involved Oedipus in his extreme calamities: for it was to try and find out his extraction that he left Corinth and met Laius, and killed him, and got his kingdom, and married his own mother, and when he then seemed at the acme of felicity, he must needs make further inquiries about himself; and though his wife tried to prevent him, he none the less compelled the old man that had been an eye-witness of the deed to tell him all the circumstances of it, and though he long suspected how the story would end, yet when the old man cried out,

> *"Alas! the dreadful tale I must then tell,"*

so inflamed was he with curiosity and trembling with impatience, that he replied,

> *"I too must hear, for hear it now I will."*

So bitter-sweet and uncontrollable is the itch of curiosity, like a sore, shedding its blood when lanced. But he that is free from this disease, and calm by nature, being ignorant of many unpleasant things, may say,

> *"Holy oblivion of all human ills,*
> *What wisdom dost thou bring!"*

It was nothing but his curiosity that involved Oedipus in his extreme calamities.

XV. We ought therefore also to accustom ourselves, when we receive a letter, not to be in a tremendous hurry about breaking the seal, as most people are, even tearing it open with their teeth if their hands are slow; nor to rise from our seat and run up to meet him, if a messenger comes; and if a friend says, "I have some news to tell you," we ought to say, "I had rather you had something useful or advantageous to tell me." When I was on one occasion lecturing at Rome, one of my audience was the well-known Rusticus, whom the Emperor Domitian afterwards had put to death through envy of his glory, and a soldier came in in the middle and brought him a letter from the Emperor, and silence ensuing, and I stopping that he might have time to read his letter, he would not, and did not open it till I had finished my lecture, and the audience had dispersed; so that everybody marvelled at his self-control. But whenever anyone who has power feeds his curiosity till it is strong and vehement, he can no longer easily control it, when it hurries him on to illicit acts, from force of habit; and such people open their friends' letters, thrust themselves in at private meetings, become spectators of rites they ought not to witness, enter holy grounds they ought not to, and pry into the lives and conversations of kings.

Whenever anyone who has power feeds his curiosity till it is strong and vehement, he can no longer easily control it.

XVI. Indeed tyrants themselves, who must know all things, are made unpopular by no class more than by their spies and talebearers. Darius in his youth, when he mistrusted his own powers, and suspected and feared everybody, was the first who employed spies; and the Dionysiuses introduced them at Syracuse: but in a revolution they were the first that the Syracusans took and tortured to death. Indeed informers are of the same tribe and family as curious people. However informers only investigate wicked acts or plots, but curious people pry into and publish abroad the involuntary misfortunes of their neighbours. And it is said that impious people first got their name from curiosity, for it seems there was a mighty famine at Athens, and those people that had wheat not producing it, but grinding it stealthily by night in their houses, some of their neighbours went about and noticed the noise of the mills grinding, and so they got their name. This also is the origin of the well-known Greek word for informer, (Sycophant, *quasi* Fig-informer), for when the people were forbidden to export figs, those who informed against those who did were called Fig-informers. It is well worth the while of curious people to give their attention to this, that they may be ashamed of having any similarity or connection in habit with a class of people so universally hated and disliked as informers.

ON SHYNESS.

ome of the things that grow on the earth are in their nature wild and barren and injurious to the growth of seeds and plants, yet those who till the ground consider them indications not of a bad soil but of a rich and fat one; so also there are passions of the soul that are not good, yet are as it were offshoots of a good disposition, and one likely to improve with good advice. Among these I class shyness, no bad sign in itself, though it affords occasion to vice. For the modest oftentimes plunge into the same excesses as the shameless, but then they are pained and grieved at them, and not pleased like the others. For the shameless person is quite apathetic at what is disgraceful, while the modest person is easily affected even at the very appearance of it. Shyness is in fact an excess of modesty. And thus it is called shamefacedness, because the face exhibits the changes of the mind. For as dejection is defined to be the grief that makes people look on the ground, so shamefacedness is that shyness that cannot look people in the face. And so the orator said the shameless person had not pupils in his eyes but harlots. The bashful person on the other hand shows his delicacy and effeminacy of soul in his countenance, and palliates his weakness, which exposes him to defeat at the hands of the impudent, by the name of modesty. Cato used to say he was better pleased with those lads that blushed than with those that turned pale, rightly

teaching us to fear censure more than labour, and suspicion than danger. However we must avoid too much timidity and fear of censure, since many have played the coward, and abandoned noble ventures, more from fear of a bad name than of the dangers to be undergone, not being able to bear a bad reputation.

II. As we must not disregard their weakness, so neither again must we praise that rigid and stubborn insensibility, "that recklessness and frantic energy to rush anywhere, that seemed like a dog's courage in Anaxarchus." But we must contrive a harmonious blending of the two, that shall remove the shamelessness of pertinacity, and the weakness of excessive modesty; seeing its cure is difficult, and the correction of such excesses not without danger. For as the husbandman, in rooting up some wild and useless weed, at once plunges his spade vigorously into the ground, and digs it up by the root, or burns it with fire, but if he has to do with a vine that needs pruning, or some apple-tree, or olive, he puts his hand to it very carefully, being afraid of injuring any sound part; so the philosopher, eradicating from the soul of the young man that ignoble and untractable weed, envy, or unseasonable avarice, or amputating the excessive love of pleasure, may bandage and draw blood, make deep incision, and leave scars: but if he has to apply reason as a corrective to a tender and delicate part of the soul, such as shyness and bashfulness, he is careful that he may not inadvertently root up modesty as well. For nurses who are often rubbing the dirt off their infants sometimes tear their flesh and put them to torture. We ought not therefore, by rubbing off the shyness of youths too much, to make them too careless and contemptuous; but as those that pull down houses close to temples prop up the adjacent parts, so in trying to get rid of shyness we must not eradicate with it the virtues akin to it, as modesty and meekness and mildness, by

In trying to get rid of shyness we must not eradicate with it the virtues akin to it.

which it insinuates itself and becomes part of a man's character, flattering the bashful man that he has a nature courteous and civil and affable, and not hard as flint or self-willed. And so the Stoics from the outset verbally distinguished shame and shyness from modesty, that they might not by identity of name give the vice opportunity to inflict harm. But let it be granted to us to use the words indiscriminately, following indeed the example of Homer. For he said,

"Modesty does both harm and good to men;"

and he did well to mention the harm it does first. For it becomes advantageous only through reason's curtailing its excess, and reducing it to moderate proportions.

III. In the first place, then, the person who is afflicted with shyness ought to be persuaded that he suffers from an injurious disease, and that nothing injurious can be good: nor must he be wheedled and tickled with the praise of being called a nice and jolly fellow rather than being styled lofty and dignified and just; nor, like Pegasus in Euripides, "who stooped and crouched lower than he wished" to take up his rider Bellerophon, must he humble himself and grant whatever favours are asked him, fearing to be called hard and ungentle. They say that the Egyptian Bocchoris, who was by nature very severe, had an asp sent him by Isis, which coiled round his head, and shaded him from above, that he might judge righteously. Bashfulness on the contrary, like a dead weight on languid and effeminate persons, not daring to refuse or contradict anybody, makes jurors deliver unjust verdicts, and shuts the mouth of counsellors, and makes people say and do many things against their wish; and so the most headstrong person is always master and lord of such, through his own impudence

The Stoics from the outset verbally distinguished shame and shyness from modesty.

prevailing against their modesty. So bashfulness, like soft and sloping ground, being unable to repel or avert any attack, lies open to the most shameful acts and passions. It is a bad guardian of youth, as Brutus said he didn't think that person had spent his youth well who had not learnt how to say No. It is a bad duenna of the bridal bed and of women's apartments, as the penitent adultress in Sophocles said to her seducer,

"You did persuade, and coax me into sin."

Shyness, being first seduced by vice, leaves its citadel unbarred, unfortified, and open to attack.

Thus shyness, being first seduced by vice, leaves its citadel unbarred, unfortified, and open to attack. By gifts people ensnare the worse natures, but by persuasion and playing upon their bashfulness people often seduce even good women. I pass over the injury done to worldly affairs by bashfulness causing people to lend to those whose credit is doubtful, and to go security against their wish, for though they commend that saying, "Be a surety, trouble is at hand," they cannot apply it when business is on hand.

IV. It would not be easy to enumerate how many this vice has ruined. When Creon said to Medea,

"Lady, 'tis better now to earn your hate,
Than through my softness afterwards to groan,"

he uttered a pregnant maxim for others; for he himself was overcome by his bashfulness, and granted her one day more, and so was the undoing of his family. And some, when they suspected murder or poison, have failed through it to take precautions for their safety. Thus perished Dion, not ignorant that Callippus was plotting against him, but ashamed to be on his guard against a friend and host. So Antipater, the son of Cassander, having invited Demetrius to supper, and being invited back by him for the next day, was ashamed to doubt another as he had been trusted himself, and went, and got his throat cut after supper. And Polysperchon promised Cassander for a hundred talents to murder Hercules, the son of Alexander by Barsine, and invited him to supper, and, as the stripling suspected and feared the invitation, and pleaded as an excuse that he was not very well, Polysperchon called on him, and addressed him as follows, "Imitate, my lad, your father's good-nature and kindness to his friends, unless indeed you fear us as plotting against you." The young man was ashamed to refuse any longer, so he went with him, and some of those at the supper-party strangled him. And so that line of Hesiod,

"Invite your friend to supper, not your enemy,"

is not ridiculous, as some say, or stupid advice, but wise. Show no bashfulness in regard to an enemy, and do not suppose him trustworthy, though he may seem so. For if you invite you will be invited back, and if you entertain others you will be entertained back to your hurt, if you let the temper as it were of your caution be weakened by shame.

V. As then this disease is the cause of much mischief, we must try and exterminate it by assiduous effort, beginning first, as people are wont to do in other matters, with small and easy things. For example, if anyone pledge you to drink with him at a dinner when you have had enough, do not be bashful, or do violence to nature, but put the cup down without drinking. Again, if somebody else challenge you to play at dice with him in your cups, be not bashful or afraid of ridicule, but imitate Xenophanes, who, when

Imitate Xenophanes, who, when Lasus called him coward because he would not play at dice with him, admitted that he had no courage for what was ignoble.

65

Diogenes used to go round begging to the statues in the Ceramicus, and when people expressed their astonishment said he was practising how to bear refusals.

Lasus of Hermione called him coward because he would not play at dice with him, admitted that he was a great coward and had no courage for what was ignoble. Again, if you meet with some prating fellow who attacks you and sticks to you, do not be bashful, but get rid of him, and hasten on and pursue your undertaking. For such flights and repulses, keeping you in practice in trying to overcome your bashfulness in small matters, will prepare you for greater occasions. And here it is well to record a remark of Demosthenes. When the Athenians were going to help Harpalus, and to war against Alexander, all of a sudden Philoxenus, who was Alexander's admiral, was sighted in the offing. And the populace being greatly alarmed, and speechless for fear, Demosthenes said, "What will they do when they see the sun, if they cannot lift their eyes to face a lamp?" And what will you do in important matters, if the king desires anything, or the people importune you, if you cannot decline to drink when your friend asks you, or evade the onset of some prating fellow, but allow the trifler to waste all your time, from not having nerve to say, "I will see you some other time, I have no leisure now."

VI. Moreover, the use and practice of restraining one's bashfulness in small and unimportant matters is advantageous also in regard to praise. For example, if a friend's harper sings badly at a drinking party, or an actor hired at great cost murders Menander, and most of the party clap and applaud, I find it by no means hard, or bad manners, to listen silently, and not to be so illiberal as to praise contrary to one's convictions. For if in such matters you are not master of yourself, what will you do if your friend reads a poor poem, or parades a speech stupidly and ridiculously written? You will praise it of course, and join the flatterers in loud applause. But how then will you find fault with your friend if he makes mistakes in business? How will you be able to correct him, if he acts improperly in reference to some office, or marriage, or the state? For I cannot indeed assent to the remark of Pericles to his friend, who asked him to bear false witness in his favour even to the extent of perjury, "I am your friend as far as the altar." He went too far. But he that has long accustomed himself never to go against his convictions in praising a speaker, or clapping a singer, or laughing at a dull buffoon, will never go to this length, nor say to some impudent fellow in such matters, "Swear on my behalf, bear false witness, pronounce an unjust verdict."

VII. So also we ought to refuse people that want to borrow money of us, from being accustomed to say *No* in small and easily refused matters. Thus Archelaus, king of the Macedonians, being asked at supper for a gold cup by a man who thought Receive the finest word in the language, bade a boy give it to Euripides, and gazing intently on the man said to him, "You are fit to ask, and not to receive, and he is fit to receive without asking." Thus did he make judgement and not bashfulness the arbiter of his gifts and favours. Yet we oftentimes pass over our friends who are both deserving and in need, and give to others who continually and impudently importune us, not from the wish to give but from the inability to say No. So the older Antigonus, being frequently annoyed by Bion, said, "Give a talent to Bion and necessity." Yet he was of all the kings most clever and ingenious at getting rid of such importunity. For on one occasion, when a Cynic asked him for a drachma, he replied, "That would be too little for a king to give;" and when the Cynic rejoined, "Give me then a talent," he met him with, "That would be too much for a Cynic to receive." Diogenes indeed used to go round begging to the statues in the Ceramicus, and when people expressed their astonishment said he was practising how to bear refusals. And we must practise

It is the fate of bashfulness, in fleeing from the smoke of ill-repute, to throw itself into the fire of it.

ourselves in small matters, and exercise ourselves in little things, with a view to refusing people who importune us, or would receive from us when inconvenient, that we may be able to avoid great miscarriages. For no one, as Demosthenes says, if he expends his resources on unnecessary things, will have means for necessary ones. And our disgrace is greatly increased, if we are deficient in what is noble, and abound in what is trivial.

VIII. But bashfulness is not only a bad and inconsiderate manager of money, but also in more important matters makes us reject expediency and reason. For when we are ill we do not call in the experienced doctor, because we stand in awe of the family one; and instead of the best teachers for our boys we select those that importune us; and in our suits at law we frequently refuse the aid of some skilled advocate, to oblige the son of some friend or relative, and give him a chance to make a forensic display; and lastly, you will find many so-called philosophers Epicureans or Stoics, not from deliberate choice or conviction, but simply from bashfulness, to have the same views as their friends and acquaintances. Since this is the case, let us accustom ourselves betimes in small and everyday matters to employ no barber or fuller merely from bashfulness, nor to put up at a sorry inn, when a better is at hand, merely because the innkeeper has on several occasions been extra civil to us, but for the benefit of the habit to select the best even in a small matter; as the Pythagoreans were careful never to put their left leg across the right, nor to take an even number instead of an odd, all other matters being indifferent. We must accustom ourselves also, at a sacrifice or marriage or any entertainment of that kind, not to invite the person who greets us and runs up to meet us, but the friend who is serviceable to us. For he that has thus practised and trained himself will be difficult to catch tripping, nay even unassailable, in greater matters.

It is well to have at hand and frequently on our lips the sayings of good and famous men to quote to those who importune us.

On Contentedness of Mind

IX. Let so much suffice for practice. And of useful considerations the first is that which teaches and reminds us, that all passions and maladies of the soul are accompanied by the very things which we think we avoid through them. Thus infamy comes through too great love of fame, and pain comes from love of pleasure, and plenty of work to the idle, and to the contentious defeats and losses of lawsuits. And so too it is the fate of bashfulness, in fleeing from the smoke of ill-repute, to throw itself into the fire of it. For the bashful, not venturing to say No to those that press them hard, afterwards feel shame at just rebuke, and, through standing in awe of slight blame, frequently in the end incur open disgrace. For if a friend asks some money of them, and through bashfulness they cannot refuse, a little time after they are disgraced by the facts becoming known; or if they have promised to help friends in a lawsuit, they turn round and hide their diminished heads, and run away from fear of the other side. Many also, who have accepted on behalf of a daughter or sister an unprofitable offer of marriage at the bidding of bashfulness, have afterwards been compelled to break their word, and break off the match.

X. He that said all the dwellers in Asia were slaves to one man because they could not say the one syllable No, spoke in jest and not in earnest; but bashful persons, even if they say nothing, can by raising or dropping their eyebrows decline many disagreeable and unpleasant acts of compliance. For Euripides says, "Silence is an answer to wise men," but we stand more in need of it to inconsiderate persons, for we can talk over the sensible. And indeed it is well to have at hand and frequently on our lips the sayings of good and famous men to quote to those who importune us, as that of Phocion to Antipater, "You cannot have me both as a friend and flatterer;" or his remark to the Athenians, when they

As Thucydides says, "It is not disgraceful to admit one's poverty, but it is very much so not to try to mend it."

applauded him and bade him contribute to the expenses of a festival, "I am ashamed to contribute anything to you, till I have paid yonder person my debts to him," pointing out his creditor Callicles. For, as Thucydides says, "It is not disgraceful to admit one's poverty, but it is very much so not to try to mend it." But he who through stupidity or softness is too bashful to say to anyone that importunes him,

"Stranger, no silver white is in my caves,"

but goes bail for him as it were through his promises,

"Is bound by fetters not of brass but shame."

But Persæus, when he lent a sum of money to one of his friends, had the fact duly attested by a banker in the market-place, remembering belike that line in Hesiod,

"E'en to a brother, smiling, bring you witness."

And he wondering and saying, "Why all these legal forms, Persæus?" he replied, "Ay, verily, that my money may be paid back in a friendly way, and that I may not have to use legal forms to get it back." For many, at first too bashful to see to security, have afterwards had to go to law, and lost their friend.

XI. Plato again, giving Helicon of Cyzicus a letter for Dionysius, praised the bearer as a man of goodness and moderation, but added at the end of the letter, "I write you this about a man, an animal by nature apt to change." But Xenocrates, though a man of austere character, was prevailed upon through his bashfulness to recommend to Polysperchon by letter, one who was no good man

Repentance follows more closely upon bashfulness than upon any emotion, and that not afterwards, but in the very act.

as the event showed; for when the Macedonian welcomed him, and inquired if he wanted any money, he asked for a talent, and Polysperchon gave it him, but wrote to Xenocrates advising him for the future to be more careful in the choice of people he recommended. But Xenocrates knew not the fellow's true character; we on the other hand very often when we know that such and such men are bad, yet give them testimonials and money, doing ourselves injury, and not getting any pleasure for it, as people do get in the company of whores and flatterers, but being vexed and disgusted at the importunity that has upset and forced our reason. For the line

> *"I know that what I'm going to do is bad,"*

is especially applicable to people that importune us, when one is going to perjure oneself, or deliver an unjust verdict, or vote for a measure that is inexpedient, or borrow money for someone who will never pay it back.

XII. And so repentance follows more closely upon bashfulness than upon any emotion, and that not afterwards, but in the very act. For we are vexed with ourselves when we give, and ashamed when we perjure ourselves, and get ill-fame from our advocacies, and are put to the blush, when we cannot fulfil our promises. For frequently, from inability to say No, we promise impossibilities to persevering applicants, as introductions at court, and audiences with princes, from reluctance or want of nerve to say, "The king does not know us, others have his regard far more." But Lysander, when he was out of favour with Agesilaus, though he was thought to have very great influence with him owing to his great reputation, was not ashamed to dismiss suitors, and bid them go and pay their court to others who had more influence with the

Not to be able to do everything carries no disgrace with it, but to force your way to what you are unable to do is a task full of trouble.

Ask which is more disgraceful, to utter a solecism and make wry faces, or to violate the law and one's oath.

king. For not to be able to do everything carries no disgrace with it, but to undertake and try and force your way to what you are unable to do, or unqualified by nature for, is in addition to the disgrace incurred a task full of trouble.

XIII. To take another element into consideration, all seemly and modest requests we ought readily to comply with, not bashfully but heartily, whereas in injurious or unreasonable requests we ought ever to remember the conduct of Zeno, who, meeting a young man he knew walking very quietly near a wall, and learning from him that he was trying to get out of the way of a friend who wanted him to perjure himself on his behalf, said to him, "O stupid fellow, what do you tell me? Is he not afraid or ashamed to press you to what is not right? And dare not you stand up boldly against him for what is right?" For he that said "villainy is no bad weapon against villainy" taught people the bad practice of standing on one's defence against vice by imitating it; but to get rid of those who shamelessly and unblushingly importune us by their own effrontery, and not to gratify the immodest in their disgraceful desires through false modesty, is the right and proper conduct of sensible people.

XIV. Moreover it is no great task to resist disreputable and low and worthless fellows who importune you, but some send such off with a laugh or a jest, as Theocritus did, who, when two fellows in the public baths, one a stranger, the other a well-known thief, wanted to borrow his scraper, put them both off with a playful answer, "You, sir, I don't know, and you I know too well." And Lysimache, the priestess of Athene Polias at Athens, when some muleteers that bore the sacred vessels asked her to give them a drink, answered, "I hesitate to do so from fear that you would make a practice of it." And when a certain young man, the son of a distinguished officer, but himself effeminate and far from bold, asked Antigonus for promotion, he replied, "With me, young man, honours are given for personal prowess, not for the prowess of ancestors."

XV. But if the person that importunes us be famous or a man of power, for such persons are very hard to move by entreaty or to get rid of when they come to sue for your vote and interest, it will not perhaps be easy or even necessary to behave as Cato, when quite a young man, did to Catulus. Catulus was in the highest repute at Rome, and at that time held the office of censor, and went to Cato, who then held the office of quæstor, and tried to beg off someone whom he had fined, and was urgent and even violent in his petitions, till Cato at last lost all patience, and said, "To have you, the censor, removed by my officers against your will, Catulus, would not be a seemly thing for you." So Catulus felt ashamed, and went off in a rage. But see whether the answers of Agesilaus and Themistocles are not more modest and in better form. Agesilaus, when he was asked by his father to pronounce sentence contrary to the law, said, "Father, I was taught by you even from my earliest years to obey the laws, so now I shall obey you and do nothing contrary to law." And Themistocles, when Simonides asked him to do something unjust, replied, "Neither would you be a good poet if your lines violated the laws of metre, nor should I be a good magistrate if I gave decisions contrary to law."

If a man of good repute tries to force and importune us to something bad, let us tell him that he is acting in an ignoble way.

XVI. And yet it is not on account of want of metrical harmony in respect to the lyre, to borrow the words of Plato, that cities quarrel with cities and friends with friends, and do and suffer the worst woes, but on account of deviations from law and justice. And yet some, who themselves pay great attention to melody and letters and measures, do not think it wrong for others to neglect what is right in magistracies and judicial sentences and business generally. One must therefore deal with them in the following manner. Does an orator ask a favour of you when you are acting as juryman, or a demagogue when you are sitting in council? Say you will grant his request if he first utter a solecism, or introduce a barbarism into his speech; he will refuse because of the shame that would attach itself to him; at any rate we see some that will not in a speech let two vowels come together. If again some illustrious and distinguished person importune you to something bad, bid him come into the market-place dancing or making wry faces, and if he refuse you will have an opportunity to speak, and ask him which is more disgraceful, to utter a solecism and make wry faces, or to violate the law and one's oath, and contrary to justice to do more for a bad than for a good man. Nicostratus the Argive, when Archidamus offered him a large sum of money and any Lacedæmonian bride he chose if he would deliver up Cromnum, said Archidamus could not be a descendant of Hercules, for he travelled about and killed evil-doers, whereas Archidamus tried to make evil-doers of the good. In like manner, if a man of good repute tries to force and importune us to something bad, let us tell him that he is acting in an ignoble way, and not as his birth and virtue would warrant.

We ought to be stout and resolute, neither yielding to bullying nor cajolery.

XVII. But in the case of people of no repute you must see whether you can persuade the miser by your importunity to lend you money without a bond, or the proud man to yield you the better place, or the ambitious man to surrender some office to you when he might take it himself. For truly it would seem monstrous that, while such remain firm and inflexible and unmoveable in their vicious propensities, we who wish to be, and profess to be, men of honour and justice should be so little masters of ourselves as to abandon and betray virtue. For indeed, if those who importune us do it for glory and power, it is absurd that we should adorn and aggrandize others only to get infamy and a bad name ourselves; like unfair umpires in the public games, or like people voting only to ingratiate themselves, and so bestowing improperly offices and prizes and glory on others, while they rob themselves of respect and fair fame. And if we see that the person who importunes us only does so for money, does it not occur to one that it is monstrous to be prodigal of one's own fame and reputation merely to make somebody else's purse heavier? Why the idea must occur to most people, they sin with their eyes open; like people who are urged hard to toss off big bumpers, and grunt and groan and make wry faces, but at last do as they are told.

XVIII. Such weakness of mind is like a temperament of body equally susceptible to heat and cold; for if such people are praised by those that importune them they are overcome and yield at once, whereas they are mortally afraid of the blame and suspicions of those whose desires they do not comply with. But we ought to be stout and resolute in either case, neither yielding to bullying nor cajolery. Thucydides indeed tells us, since envy necessarily follows ability, that "he is well advised who incurs envy in matters of the highest importance." But we, thinking it difficult to escape envy, and seeing that it is altogether impossible not to incur blame or give offence to those we live with, shall be well advised if we prefer the hatred of the perverse to that of those who might justly find fault with us for having iniquitously served their turn. And indeed we ought to be on our guard against praise from those who importune us, which is sure to be altogether insincere, and not to resemble swine, readily allowing anyone that presses to make use of us from our pleasure at itching and tickling, and submitting ourselves to their will. For those that give their ears to flatterers

Thucydides tells us, since envy necessarily follows ability, that "he is well advised who incurs envy in matters of the highest importance."

differ not a whit from such as let themselves be tripped up at wrestling, only their overthrow and fall is more disgraceful; some forbearing hostility and reproof in the case of bad men, that they may be called merciful and humane and compassionate; and others on the contrary persuaded to take up unnecessary and dangerous animosities and charges by those who praise them as the only men, the only people that never flatter, and go so far as to entitle them their mouthpieces and voices. Accordingly Bio compared such people to jars, that you could easily take by the ears and turn about at your will. Thus it is recorded that the sophist Alexinus in one of his lectures said a good many bad things about Stilpo the Megarian, but when one of those that were present said, "Why, he was speaking in your praise only the other day," he replied, "I don't doubt it; for he is the best and noblest of men." Menedemus on the contrary, having heard that Alexinus frequently praised him, replied, "But I always censure him, for that man is bad who either praises a bad man or is blamed by a good." So inflexible and proof was he against such flattery, and master of that advice which Hercules in Antisthenes gave, when he ordered his sons to be grateful to no one that praised them; which meant nothing else than that they should not be dumbfounded at it, nor flatter again those who praised them. Very apt, I take it, was the remark of Pindar to one who told him that he praised him everywhere and to all persons, "I am greatly obliged to you, and will make your account true by my actions."

XIX. A useful precept in reference to all passions is especially valuable in the case of the bashful. When they have been overcome by this infirmity, and against their judgement have erred and been confounded, let them fix it in their memories, and, remembering the pain and grief it gave them, let them recall it to their mind and be on their guard for a very long time. For as

Those that give their ears to flatterers differ not a whit from such as let themselves be tripped up at wrestling, only their overthrow and fall is more disgraceful.

travellers that have stumbled against a stone, or pilots that have been wrecked off a headland, if they remember these occurrences, not only dread and are on their guard continually on those spots, but also on all similar ones; so those that frequently remember the disgrace and injury that bashfulness brought them, and its sorrow and anguish, will in similar cases be on their guard against their weakness, and will not readily allow themselves to be subjugated by it again.

On Restraining Anger.
A Dialogue Between Sylla and Fundanus.

 ylla. Those painters, Fundanus, seem to me to do well who, before giving the finishing touches to their paintings, lay them by for a time and then revise them; because by taking their eyes off them for a time they gain by frequent inspection a new insight, and are more apt to detect minute differences, that continuous familiarity would have hidden. Now since a human being cannot so separate himself from himself for a time, and make a break in his continuity, and then approach himself again—and that is perhaps the chief reason why a man is a worse judge of himself than of others—the next best thing will be for a man to inspect his friends after an interval, and likewise offer himself to their scrutiny, not to see whether he has aged quickly, or whether his bodily condition is better or worse, but to examine his moral character, and see whether time has added any good quality, or removed any bad one. On my return then to Rome after an absence of two years, and having been with you now five months, I am not at all surprised that there has been a great increase and growth in those good points which you formerly had owing to your admirable nature; but when I see how gentle and obedient to reason your former excessive impetuosity and hot temper has become, it cannot but occur to me to quote the line,

"Ye gods, how much more mild is he become!"

And this mildness has not wrought in you sloth or weakness, but like cultivation of the soil it has produced a smoothness and depth fit for action, instead of the former impetuosity and vehemence. And so it is clear that your propensity to anger has not been effaced by any declining vigour or through some chance, but has been cured by good precepts. And indeed, for I will tell you the truth, when our friend Eros reported this change in you to me, I suspected that owing to goodwill he bare witness not of the actual state of the case, but of what was becoming to all good and virtuous men, although, as you know, he can never be persuaded to depart from his real opinion to ingratiate himself with anyone. But now he is acquitted of false witness, and do you, as your journey gives you leisure, narrate to me the mode of cure you employed to make your temper so under control, so natural, gentle and obedient to reason.

Fundanus. Most friendly Sylla, take care that you do not in your goodwill and affection to me rest under any misconception of my real condition. For it is possible that Eros, not being able always himself to keep his temper in its place in the obedience that Homer speaks of, but sometimes carried away by his hatred of what is bad, may think me grown milder than I really am, as in changes of the scale in music the lowest notes become the highest.

Sylla. Neither of these is the case, Fundanus, but oblige me by doing as I ask.

II. *Fundanus.* One of the excellent precepts then of Musonius that I remember, Sylla, is this, that those who wish to be well should diet themselves all their life long. For I do not think we

Anger, like a fortified tyranny, must have someone born and bred within it to overthrow it.

must employ reason as a cure, as we do hellebore, by purging it out with the disease, but we must retain it in the soul, to restrain and govern the judgement. For the power of reason is not like physic, but wholesome food, which co-operates with good health in producing a good habit of body in those by whom it is taken. But admonition and reproof, when passion is at its height and swelling, does little or no good, but resembles very closely those strong-smelling substances, that are able to set on their legs again those that have fallen in epileptic fits, but cannot rid them of their disease. For although all other passions, even at the moment of their acme, do in some sort listen to reason and admit it into the soul, yet anger does not, for, as Melanthius says,

"Fell things it does when it the mind unsettles,"

for it absolutely turns reason out of doors, and bolts it out, and, like those persons who burn themselves and houses together, it makes all the interior full of confusion and smoke and noise, so that what would be advantageous can neither be seen nor heard. And so an empty ship in a storm at open sea would sooner admit on board a pilot from without, than a man in a tempest of rage and anger would listen to another's advice, unless his own reason was first prepared to hearken. But as those who expect a siege get together and store up supplies, when they despair of relief from without, so ought we by all means to scour the country far and wide to derive aids against anger from philosophy, and store them up in the soul: for, when the time of need comes, we shall find it no easy task to import them. For either the soul doesn't hear what is said without because of the uproar, if it have not within its own reason (like a boatswain as it were) to receive at once and understand every exhortation; or if it does hear, it despises what is uttered mildly and gently, while it is exasperated by harsh censure.

Anger is not only appeased by the sprinkling of cold water, but is also extinguished by the action of fear.

For anger being haughty and self-willed and hard to be worked upon by another, like a fortified tyranny, must have someone born and bred within it to overthrow it.

III. Now long-continued anger, and frequent giving way to it, produces an evil disposition of soul, which people call irascibility, and which ends in passionateness, bitterness, and peevishness, whenever the mind becomes sore and vexed at trifles and querulous at everyday occurrences, like iron thin and beaten out too fine. But when the judgement checks and suppresses at once the rising anger, it not only cures the soul for the moment, but restores its tone and balance for the future. It has happened to myself indeed twice or thrice, when I strongly fought against anger, that I was in the same plight as the Thebans, who after they had once defeated the Lacedæmonians, whom they had hitherto thought invincible, never lost a battle against them again. I then felt confident that reason can win the victory. I saw also that anger is not only appeased by the sprinkling of cold water, as Aristotle attested, but is also extinguished by the action of fear; aye, and, as Homer tells us, anger has been cured and has melted away in the case of many by some sudden joy. So that I came to the conclusion that this passion is not incurable for those who wish to be cured. For it does not arise from great and important causes, but banter and joking, a laugh or a nod, and similar trifles make many angry, as Helen by addressing her niece,

> *"Electra, maiden now for no short time,"*

provoked her to reply,

> *"Your wisdom blossoms late, since formerly*
> *You left your house in shame;"*

He that observes anger in its rise, and sees it gradually smoking and bursting forth into fire, can frequently smother it merely by silence.

and Callisthenes incensed Alexander, by saying, when a huge cup was brought to him, "I will not drink to Alexander till I shall require the help of Æsculapius."

IV. As then it is easy to put out a flame kindled in the hair of hares and in wicks and rubbish, but if it once gets hold of things solid and thick, it quickly destroys and consumes them, "raging amidst the lofty work of the carpenters," as Æschylus says; so he that observes anger in its rise, and sees it gradually smoking and bursting forth into fire from some chatter or rubbishy scurrility, need have no great trouble with it, but can frequently smother it merely by silence and contempt. For as a person puts out a fire by bringing no fuel to it, so with respect to anger, he that does not in the beginning fan it, and stir up its rage in himself, keeps it off and destroys it. And so, though Hieronymus has given us many useful sayings and precepts, I am not pleased with his remark that there is no perception of anger in its birth, but only in its actual developement, so quick is it. For none of the passions when stirred up and set in motion has so palpable a birth and growth as anger. As indeed Homer skilfully shows us, where he represents Achilles as seized at once with grief, when word was brought him of Patroclus' death, in the line,

"Thus spake he, and grief's dark cloud covered him;"

whereas he represents him as waxing angry with Agamemnon slowly, and as inflamed by his many words, which if either of them had abstained from, their quarrel would not have attained such growth and magnitude. And so Socrates, as often as he perceived any anger rising in him against any of his friends, "setting himself like some ocean promontory to break the violence of the waves," would lower his voice, and put on a smiling countenance, and give

Socrates would lower his voice, and put on a smiling countenance, and give his eye a gentler expression, thus keeping himself from fall and defeat.

83

The first way to overcome anger, like the putting down of some tyrant, is not to obey or listen to it when it bids you speak loud.

his eye a gentler expression, by inclining in the other direction and running counter to his passion, thus keeping himself from fall and defeat.

V. For the first way, my friend, to overcome anger, like the putting down of some tyrant, is not to obey or listen to it when it bids you speak loud, and look fierce, and beat yourself, but to remain quiet, and not to make the passion more intense, as one would a disease, by tossing about and crying out. In love affairs indeed, such things as revellings, and serenadings, and crowning the loved one's door with garlands, may indeed bring some pleasant and elegant relief.

> "I went, but asked not who or whose she was,
> I merely kissed her door-post. If that be
> A crime, I do plead guilty to the same."

In the case of mourners also giving up to weeping and wailing takes away with the tears much of the grief. But anger on the contrary is much more fanned by what angry persons do and say. It is best therefore to be calm, or to flee and hide ourselves and go to a haven of quiet, when we feel the fit of temper coming upon us as an epileptic fit, that we fall not, or rather fall not on others, for it is our friends that we fall upon most and most frequently. For we do not love all, nor envy all, nor fear all men; but nothing is untouched or unassailed by anger; for we are angry with friends and enemies, parents and children, aye, and with the gods, and beasts, and even things inanimate, as was Thamyris,

> "Breaking his gold-bound horn, breaking the music
> Of well-compacted lyre;"

and Pandarus, who called down a curse upon himself, if he did not burn his bow "after breaking it with his hands." And Xerxes inflicted strikes and blows on the sea, and sent letters to Mount Athos, "Divine Athos, whose top reaches heaven, put not in the way of my works stones large and difficult to deal with, or else I will hew thee down, and throw thee into the sea." For anger has many formidable aspects, and many ridiculous ones, so that of all the passions it is the most hated and despised. It will be well to consider both aspects.

VI. To begin then, whether my process was wrong or right I know not, but I began my cure of anger by noticing its effects in others, as the Lacedæmonians study the nature of drunkenness in the Helots. And in the first place, as Hippocrates tells us that disease is most dangerous in which the face of the patient is most unlike himself, so observing that people beside themselves with anger change their face, colour, walk, and voice, I formed an impression as it were of that aspect of passion, and was very disgusted with myself if ever I should appear so frightful and like one out of his mind to my friends and wife and daughters, not only wild and unlike oneself in appearance, but also with a voice savage and harsh, as I had noticed in some of my acquaintance, who could neither preserve for anger their ordinary behaviour, or demeanour, or grace of language, or persuasiveness and gentleness in conversation. Caius Gracchus, indeed, the orator, whose character was harsh and style of oratory impassioned, had a pitch-pipe made for him, such as musicians use to heighten or lower their voices by degrees, and this, when he was making a speech, a slave stood behind him and held, and used to give him a mild and gentle note on it, whereby he lowered his key, and removed from his voice the harsh and passionate element, charming and laying the heat of the orator,

I began my cure of anger by noticing its effects in others.

*"As shepherds' wax-joined reed sounds musically
With sleep provoking strain."*

For myself if I had some elegant and sprightly companion, I should not be vexed at his showing me a looking-glass in my fits of anger, as they offer one to some after a bath to little useful end. For to behold oneself unnaturally distorted in countenance will condemn anger in no small degree. The poets playfully tell us that Athene when playing on the pipe was rebuked thus by a Satyr,

*"That look no way becomes you, take your armour,
Lay down your pipes, and do compose your cheeks,"*

and though she paid no attention to him, yet afterwards when she saw her face in a river, she felt vexed and threw her pipes away, although art had made melody a compensation for her unsightliness. And Marsyas, it seems, by a sort of mouthpiece forcibly repressed the violence of his breath, and tricked up and hid the contortion of his face,

*"Around his shaggy temples put bright gold,
And o'er his open mouth thongs tied behind."*

To behold oneself unnaturally distorted in countenance will condemn anger in no small degree.

Now anger, that puffs up and distends the face so as to look ugly, utters a voice still more harsh and unpleasant,

"Moving the mind's chords undisturbed before."

They say that the sea is cleansed when agitated by the winds it throws up tangle and seaweed; but the intemperate and bitter and vain words, which the mind throws up when the soul is agitated, defile the speakers of them first of all and fill them with infamy, as always having those thoughts within their bosom and being defiled with them, but only giving vent to them in anger. And so for a word which is, as Plato styles it, "a very small matter," they incur a most heavy punishment, for they get reputed to be enemies, and evil speakers, and malignant in disposition.

VII. Seeing and observing all this, it occurs to me to take it as a matter of fact, and record it for my own general use, that if it is good to keep the tongue soft and smooth in a fever, it is better to keep it so in anger. For if the tongue of people in a fever be unnatural, it is a bad sign, but not the cause of their malady; but the tongue of angry people, being rough and foul, and breaking out into unseemly speeches, produces insults that work irremediable mischief, and argue deep-rooted malevolence within. For wine drunk neat does not exhibit the soul in so ungovernable and hateful a condition as temper does: for the outbreaks of the one smack of laughter and fun, while those of the other are compounded with gall: and at a drinking-bout he that is silent is burdensome to the company and tiresome, whereas in anger nothing is more highly thought of than silence, as Sappho advises,

> "When anger's busy in the brain
> Thy idly-barking tongue restrain."

VIII. And not only does the consideration of all this naturally arise from observing ourselves in the moments of anger, but we cannot help seeing also the other properties of rage, how ignoble it is, how unmanly, how devoid of dignity and greatness of mind! And yet to most people its noise seems vigour, its threatening confidence, and its obstinacy force of character; some even not wisely entitle its savageness magnanimity, and its implacability firmness, and its morosity hatred of what is bad. For their actions

If it is good to keep the tongue soft and smooth in a fever, it is better to keep it so in anger.

and motions and whole demeanour argue great littleness and meanness, not only when they are fierce with little boys, and peevish with women, and think it right to treat dogs and horses and mules with harshness, as Otesiphon the pancratiast thought fit to kick back a mule that had kicked him, but even in the butcheries that tyrants commit their littleness of soul is apparent in their savageness, and their suffering in their action, so that they are like the bites of serpents, that, when they are burnt and smart with pain, violently thrust their venom on those that have hurt them. For as a swelling is produced in the flesh by a heavy blow, so in softest souls the inclination to hurt others gets its greater strength from greater weakness. Thus women are more prone to anger than men, and people ill than people well, and old men than men in their prime, and the unfortunate than the prosperous; the miser is most prone to anger with his steward, the glutton with his cook, the jealous man with his wife, the vain man when he is spoken ill of; and worst of all are those "men who are too eager in states for office, or to head a faction, a manifest sorrow," to borrow Pindar's words. So from the very great pain and suffering of the soul there arises mainly from weakness anger, which is not like the nerves of the soul, as someone defined it, but like its strainings and convulsions when it is excessively vehement in its thirst for revenge.

The inclination to hurt others gets its greater strength from greater weakness.

IX. Such bad examples as these were not pleasant to look at but necessary, but I shall now proceed to describe people who have been mild and easy in dealing with anger, conduct gratifying either to see or hear about, being utterly disgusted with people who use such language as,

"You have a man wronged: shall a man stand this?"

and,

> *"Put your heel upon his neck, and dash his head against the ground,"*

and other provoking expressions such as these, by which some not well have transferred anger from the woman's side of the house to the man's. For manliness in all other respects seems to resemble justice, and to differ from it only in respect to gentleness, with which it has more affinities. For it sometimes happens to worse men to govern better ones, but to erect a trophy in the soul against anger (which Heraclitus says it is difficult to contend against, for whatever it wishes is bought at the price of the soul), is a proof of power so great and victorious as to be able to apply the judgement as if it were nerves and sinews to the passions. So I always try to collect and peruse the remarks on this subject not only of the philosophers, who foolish people say had no gall in their composition, but still more of kings and tyrants. Such was the remark of Antigonus to his soldiers, when they were abusing him near his tent as if he were not listening, so he put his staff out, and said, "What's to do? can you not go rather farther off to run me down?" And when Arcadio the Achæan, who was always railing against Philip, and advising people to flee

> *"Unto a country where they knew not Philip,"*

visited Macedonia afterwards on some chance or other, the king's friends thought he ought to be punished and the matter not looked over; but Philip treated him kindly, and sent him presents and gifts, and afterwards bade inquiry to be made as to what sort of account of him Arcadio now gave to the Greeks; and when all testified that the fellow had become a wonderful praiser of the

Ptolemy said, "If it is not kingly to take a flout, neither is it kingly to give one."

Bravery has no need of gall, being dipped in reason.

king, Philip said, "You see I knew how to cure him better than all of you." And at the Olympian games when there was defamation of Philip, and some of his suite said to him, that the Greeks ought to smart for it, because they railed against him when they were treated well by him, he replied, "What will they do then if they are treated badly by me?" Excellent also was the behaviour of Pisistratus to Thrasybulus, and of Porsena to Mucius, and of Magas to Philemon. As to Magas, after he had been publicly jeered at by Philemon in one of his comedies at the theatre in the following words,

> *"Magas, the king hath written thee a letter,*
> *Unhappy Magas, since thou can'st not read,"*

after having taken Philemon, who had been cast on shore by a storm at Parætonium, he commanded one of his soldiers only to touch his neck with the naked sword and then to go away quietly, and dismissed him, after sending him a ball and some dice as if he were a silly boy. And Ptolemy on one occasion, flouting a grammarian for his ignorance, asked him who was the father of Peleus, and he answered, "I will tell you, if you tell me first who was the father of Lagus." This was a jeer at the obscure birth of the king, and all his courtiers were indignant at it as an unpardonable liberty; but Ptolemy said, "If it is not kingly to take a flout, neither is it kingly to give one." And Alexander was more savage than usual in his behaviour to Callisthenes and Clitus. So Porus, when he was taken captive, begged Alexander to use him as a king. And on his inquiring, "What, nothing more?" he replied, "No. For everything is included in being used as a king." So they call the king of the gods Milichius, while they call Ares Maimactes; and punishment and torture they assign to the Erinnyes and to demons, not to the gods or Olympus.

On Contentedness of Mind

X. As then a certain person passed the following remark on Philip when he had razed Olynthus to the ground, "He certainly could not build such another city," so we may say to anger, "You can root up, and destroy, and throw down, but to raise up and save and spare and tolerate is the work of mildness and moderation, the work of a Camillus, a Metellus, an Aristides, a Socrates; but to sting and bite is to resemble the ant and horse-fly. For, indeed, when I consider revenge, I find its angry method to be for the most part ineffectual, since it spends itself in biting the lips and gnashing the teeth, and in vain attacks, and in railings coupled with foolish threats, and eventually resembles children running races, who from feebleness ridiculously tumble down before they reach the goal they are hastening to. So that speech of the Rhodian to a lictor of the Roman prætor who was shouting and talking insolently was not inapt, "It is no matter to me what you say, but what your master thinks." And Sophocles, when he had introduced Neoptolemus and Eurypylus as armed for the battle, gives them this high commendation,

Hunters and orators are very unsuccessful when they give way to anger.

"They rushed into the midst of armed warriors."

Some barbarians indeed poison their steel, but bravery has no need of gall, being dipped in reason, but rage and fury are not invincible but rotten. And so the Lacedæmonians by their pipes turn away the anger of their warriors, and sacrifice to the Muses before commencing battle, that reason may abide with them, and when they have routed a foe do not follow up the victory, but relax their rage, which like small daggers they can easily take back. But anger kills myriads before it is glutted with revenge, as happened in the case of Cyrus and Pelopidas the Theban. But Agathocles bore mildly the revilings of those he was besieging, and when one of them cried out, "Potter, how are you going to get money to pay your mercenaries?" he replied laughingly, "Out of your town if I take it." And when some of those on the wall threw his ugliness into the teeth of Antigonus, he said to them, "I thought I was rather a handsome fellow." But after he had taken the town, he sold for slaves those that had flouted him, protesting that, if they insulted him again, he would bring the matter before their masters. I have noticed also that hunters and orators are very unsuccessful when they give way to anger. And Aristotle tells us that the friends of Satyrus stopped up his ears with wax when he was to plead a cause, that he might not make any confusion in the case through rage at the abuse of his enemies. And does it not frequently happen with ourselves that a slave who has offended escapes punishment, because they abscond in fear of our threats and harsh words? What nurses then say to children, "Give up crying, and you shall have it," may usefully be applied to anger, thus, "Do not be in a hurry, or bawl out, or be vehement, and you will sooner and better get what you want." For a father, seeing his boy trying to cut or cleave something with a knife, takes the knife from him and does it himself: and similarly a person, taking revenge out of the hand of passion, does himself safely and usefully and without harm punish the person who deserves punishment, and not himself instead, as anger often does.

It is impossible to check irresponsible power, unless one wields power with much meekness.

XI. Now though all the passions need such discipline as by exercise shall tame and subdue their unreasoning and disobedient elements, yet there is none which we ought to keep under by such discipline so much as the exhibition of anger to our servants. For neither envy, nor fear, nor rivalry come into play between them and us; but our frequent displays of anger to them, creating many offences and faults, make us to slip as if on slippery ground owing to our autocracy with our servants, which no one resists or prevents. For it is impossible to check irresponsible power so as never to break out under the influence of passion, unless one wields power with much meekness, and refuses to listen to the frequent complaints of one's wife and friends charging one with being too easy and lax with one's servants. And by nothing have I been more exasperated against them, as if they were being ruined for want of correction. At last, though late, I got to see that in the first place it is better to make them worse by forbearance, than by bitterness and anger to distort oneself for the correction of others. In the next place I observed that many for the very reason that they were not corrected were frequently ashamed to be bad, and made pardon rather than punishment the commencement of their reformation, aye, and made better slaves to some merely at their nod silently and cheerfully than to others with all their beatings and brandings, and so I came to the conclusion that reason gets better obeyed than temper, for it is not as the poet said,

"Where there is fear, there too is self-respect,"

but it is just the other way about, for self-respect begets that kind of fear that corrects the behaviour. But perpetual and pitiless beating produces not so much repentance for wrong-doing as contrivances to continue in it without detection. In the third place, ever remembering and reflecting within myself that, just as he that teaches us the use of the bow does not forbid us to shoot but only to miss the mark, so it will not prevent punishment altogether to teach people to do it in season, and with moderation, utility, and decorum, I strive to remove anger most especially by not forbidding those who are to be corrected to speak in their defence, but by listening to them. For the interval of time gives a pause to passion, and a delay that mitigates it, and so judgement finds out both the fit manner and adequate amount of punishment. Moreover he that is punished has nothing to allege

Phocion, after the death of Alexander, to stop the Athenians from revolting, said to them, "Men of Athens, if he is dead to-day, he will certainly also be dead to-morrow."

against his correction, if he is punished not in anger but only after his guilt is brought home to him. And the greatest disgrace will not be incurred, which is when the servant seems to speak more justly than the master. As then Phocion, after the death of Alexander, to stop the Athenians from revolting and believing the news too soon, said to them, "Men of Athens, if he is dead to-day, he will certainly also be dead to-morrow and the next day," so I think the man who is in a hurry to punish anyone in his rage ought to consider with himself, "If this person has wronged you to-day, he will also have wronged you to-morrow and the next day; and there will be no harm done if he shall be punished somewhat late; whereas if he shall be punished at once, he will always seem to you to have been innocent, as has often happened before now." For which of us is so savage as to chastise and scourge a slave because five or ten days before he over-roasted the meat, or upset the table, or was somewhat tardy on some errand? And yet these are the very things for which we put ourselves out and are harsh and implacable, immediately after they have happened and are recent. For as bodies seem greater in a mist, so do little matters in a rage. We ought therefore to consider such arguments as these at once, and if, when there is no trace of passion left, the matter appear bad to calm and clear reason, then it ought to be taken in hand, and the punishment ought not to be neglected or abandoned, as we leave food when we have lost our appetites. For nothing causes people to punish so much when their anger is fierce, as that when it is appeased they do not punish at all, but forget the matter entirely, and resemble lazy rowers, who lie in harbour when the sea is calm, and then sail out to their peril when the wind gets up. So we, condemning reason for slackness and mildness in punishing, are in a hurry to punish, borne along by passion as by a dangerous gale. He that is hungry takes his food as nature dictates, but he that punishes should have

He that punishes should have no hunger or thirst for it.

no hunger or thirst for it, nor require anger as a sauce to stimulate him to it, but should punish when he is as far as possible from having any desire for it, and has to compel his reason to it. For we ought not, as Aristotle tells us slaves in his time were scourged in Etruria to the music of the flute, to go headlong into punishing with a desire and zest for it, and to delight in punishing, and then afterwards to be sorry at it—for the first is savage, and the last womanish—but we should without either sorrow or pleasure chastise at the dictates of reason, giving anger no opportunity to interfere.

XII. But this perhaps will not appear a cure of anger so much as a putting away and avoiding such faults as men commit in anger. And yet, though the swelling of the spleen is only a symptom of fever, the fever is assuaged by its abating, as Hieronymus tells us. Now when I contemplated the origin of anger itself, I observed that, though different persons fell into it for different reasons, yet in nearly all of them was the idea of their being despised and neglected to be found. So we ought to help those who try to get rid of anger, by removing as far as possible from them any action savouring of contempt or contumely, and by looking upon their anger as folly or necessity, or emotion, or mischance, as Sophocles says,

> "In those that are unfortunate, O king,
> No mind stays firm, but all their balance lose."

And so Agamemnon, ascribing to Ate his carrying off Briseis, yet says to Achilles,

> "I wish to please you in return, and give
> Completest satisfaction."

Fits of anger that gather together in the soul by degrees, like a swarm of bees, are generated within us by selfishness and peevishness.

They that require little do not miss much.

For suing is not the action of one who shews his contempt, and when he that has done an injury is humble he removes all idea of slighting one. But the angry person must not expect this, but rather take to himself the answer of Diogenes, who, when it was said to him, "These people laugh at you," replied, "But I am not one to be laughed at," and not think himself despised, but rather despise the person who gave the offence, as acting from weakness, or error, or rashness, or heedlessness, or illiberality, or old age, or youth. Nor must we entertain such notions with regard to our servants and friends. For they do not despise us as void of ability or energy, but owing to our evenness and good-nature, some because we are mild, and others presuming on our affection for them. But as it is we not only fly into rages with wife and slaves and friends, as if we were slighted by them, but we also frequently, from forming the same idea of being slighted, fall foul of innkeepers and sailors and muleteers, and are vexed at dogs that bark and asses that are in our way: like the man who was going to beat an ass-driver, but when he cried out he was an Athenian, he said to the ass, "You are not an Athenian anyway," and beat it with many strikes.

XIII. Moreover those continuous and frequent fits of anger that gather together in the soul by degrees, like a swarm of bees or wasps, are generated within us by selfishness and peevishness, luxury and softness. And so nothing causes us to be mild to our servants and wife and friends so much as easiness and simplicity, and the learning to be content with what we have, and not to require a quantity of superfluities.

> *"He who likes not his meat if over-roast*
> *Or over-boiled, or under-roast or under-boiled,*
> *And never praises it however dressed,"*

but will not drink unless he have snow to cool his drink, nor eat bread purchased in the market, nor touch food served on cheap or earthenware plates, nor sleep upon any but a feather bed that rises and falls like the sea stirred up from its depths, and with rods and blows hastens his servants at table, so that they run about and cry out and sweat as if they were bringing poultices to sores, he is slave to a weak, querulous and discontented mode of life, and, like one who has a continual cough or various ailments, whether he is aware of it or not, he is in an ulcerous and catarrh-like condition as regards his proneness to anger. We must therefore train the body to contentment by plain living, that it may be easily satisfied: for they that require little do not miss much; and it is no great hardship to begin with our food, and take it silently whatever it is, and not by being choleric and peevish to thrust upon ourselves and friends the worst sauce to meat, anger.

"No more unpleasant supper could there be"

than that wherein the servants are beaten, and the wife scolded, because something is burnt or smoked or not salt enough, or because the bread is too cold. Arcesilaus was once entertaining some friends and strangers, and when dinner was served, there was no bread, through the servants having neglected to buy any. In such a case as this which of us would not have broken the walls with vociferation? But he only smiled and said, "How unfit a sage is to give an entertainment!" And when Socrates once took Euthydemus home with him from the wrestling-school, Xanthippe was in a towering rage, and scolded, and at last upset the table, and Euthydemus rose and went away full of sorrow. But Socrates said to him, "Did not a hen at your house the other day fly in and act in the very same way? And we did not put ourselves out about it." We ought to receive our friends with gaiety and

He that is prone to anger should not use rare and dainty things, such as choice cups and seals and precious stones.

smiles and welcome, not knitting our brows, or inspiring fear and trembling in the attendants. We ought also to accustom ourselves to the use of any kind of ware at table, and not to stint ourselves to one kind rather than another, as some pick out a particular tankard or horn, as they say Marius did, out of many, and will not drink out of anything else; and some act in the same way with regard to oil-flasks and scrapers, being content with only one out of all, and so, if such an article is broken or lost, they are very much put out about it, and punish with severity. He then that is prone to anger should not use rare and dainty things, such as choice cups and seals and precious stones: for if they are lost they put a man beside himself much more than the loss of ordinary and easily got things would do. And so when Nero had got an eight-cornered tent constructed, a wonderful object both for its beauty and costliness, Seneca said to him, "You have now shown yourself to be poor, for if you should lose this, you will not be able to procure such another." And indeed it did so happen that the tent was lost by shipwreck, but Nero bore its loss patiently, remembering what Seneca had said. Now this easiness about things generally makes a man also easy and gentle to his servants, and if to them, then it is clear he will be so to his friends also, and to all that serve under him in any capacity. So we observe that newly-purchased slaves do not inquire about the master who has bought them, whether he is superstitious or envious, but only whether he is a bad-tempered man: and generally speaking we see that neither can men put up with chaste wives, nor wives with loving husbands, nor friends with one another, if they be ill-tempered to boot. So neither marriage nor friendship is bearable with anger, though without anger even drunkenness is a small matter. For the wand of Dionysus punishes sufficiently the drunken man, but if anger be added it turns wine from being the dispeller of care and inspirer of the dance into a savage and fury.

We ought to give anger no vent, either in jest or in adversity, for that deprives people of compassion.

And simple madness can be cured by Anticyra, but madness mixed with anger is the producer of tragedies and dreadful narratives.

XIV. So we ought to give anger no vent, either in jest, for that draws hatred to friendliness; or in discussion, for that turns love of learning into strife; or on the judgement-seat, for that adds insolence to power; or in teaching, for that produces dejection and hatred of learning: or in prosperity, for that increases envy; or in adversity, for that deprives people of compassion, when they are peevish and run counter to those who condole with them, like Priam,

> *"A murrain on you, worthless wretches all,*
> *Have you no griefs at home, that here you come*
> *To sympathize with me?"*

Good temper on the other hand is useful in some circumstances, adorns and sweetens others, and gets the better of all peevishness and anger by its gentleness. Thus Euclides, when his brother said to him in a dispute between them, "May I perish, if I don't have my revenge on you!" replied, "May I perish, if I don't persuade you!" and so at once turned and changed him. And Polemo, when a man reviled him who was fond of precious stones and quite crazy for costly seal-rings, made no answer, but bestowed all his attention on one of his seal-rings, and eyed it closely; and he being delighted said, "Do not look at it so, Polemo, but in the light of the sun, and it will appear to you more beautiful." And Aristippus, when there was anger between him and Æschines, and somebody said, "O Aristippus, where is now your friendship?" replied, "It is asleep, but I will wake it up," and went to Æschines, and said to him, "Do I seem to you so utterly unfortunate and incurable as to be unworthy of any consideration?" And Æschines

Anger is even worse than envy, for it does not mind its own suffering if it can only implicate another in misery.

replied, "It is not at all wonderful that you, being naturally superior to me in all things, should have been first to detect in this matter too what was needful."

> *"For not a woman only, but young child*
> *Tickling the bristly boar with tender hand,*
> *Will lay him prostrate sooner than an athlete."*

But we that tame wild beasts and make them gentle, and carry in our arms young wolves and lions' whelps, inconsistently repel our children and friends and acquaintances in our rage, and let loose our temper like some wild beast on our servants and fellow-citizens, speciously trying to disguise it not rightly under the name of hatred of evil, but it is, I suppose, as with the other passions and diseases of the soul, we cannot get rid of any of them by calling one prudence, and another liberality, and another piety.

Nothing swells the anger more, than when one who we thought loved us falls out and jangles with us.

XV. And yet, as Zeno said the seed was a mixture and compound drawn from all the faculties of the soul, so anger seems a universal seed from all the passions. For it is drawn from pain and pleasure and haughtiness, and from envy it gets its property of malignity—and it is even worse than envy, for it does not mind its own suffering if it can only implicate another in misery—and the most unlovely kind of desire is innate in it, namely the appetite for injuring another. So when we go to the houses of spendthrifts we hear a flute-playing girl early in the morning, and see "the dregs of wine," as one said, and fragments of garlands, and the servants at the doors reeking of yesterday's debauch; but for tokens of savage and peevish masters these you will see by the faces, and marks, and manacles of their servants: for in the house of an angry man

"The only music ever heard is wailing,"

stewards being beaten within, and maids tortured, so that the spectators even in their jollity and pleasure pity these victims of passion.

XVI. Moreover those to whom it happens through their genuine hatred of what is bad to be frequently overtaken by anger, can abate its excess and acerbity by giving up their excessive confidence in their intimates. For nothing swells the anger more, than when a good man is detected of villainy, or one who we thought loved us falls out and jangles with us. As for my own disposition, you know of course how mightily it inclines to goodwill and belief in mankind. As then people walking on empty space, the more confidently I believe in anybody's affection, the more sorrow and distress do I feel if my estimate is a mistaken one. And indeed I could never divest myself of my ardour and zeal in affection, but as to trusting people I could perhaps use Plato's caution as a curb. For he said he so praised Helicon the mathematician, because he was by nature a changeable animal, but that he was afraid of those that were well educated in the city, lest, being human beings and the seed of human beings, they should reveal by some trait or other the weakness of human nature. But Sophocles' line,

"Trace out most human acts, you'll find them base,"

It is the sudden and unexpected that makes people go distracted.

seems to trample on human nature and lower its merits too much. Still such a peevish and condemnatory verdict as this has a tendency to make people milder in their rage, for it is the sudden and unexpected that makes people go distracted. And we ought, as Panætius somewhere said, to imitate Anaxagoras, and as he said

As small writing strains the eyes, so small matters even more strain and bother people.

at the death of his son, "I knew that I had begotten a mortal," so ought every one of us to use the following kind of language in those contretemps that stir up our anger, "I knew that the slave I bought was not a philosopher," "I knew that the friend I had was not perfect," "I knew that my wife was but a woman." And if anyone would also constantly put to himself that question of Plato, "Am I myself all I should be?" and look at home instead of abroad, and curb his propensity to censoriousness, he would not be so keen to detect evil in others, for he would see that he stood in need of much allowance himself. But now each of us, when angry and punishing, quote the words of Aristides and Cato, "Do not steal, Do not tell lies," and "Why are you lazy?" And, what is most disgraceful of all, we blame angry people when we are angry ourselves, and chastise in temper faults that were committed in temper, unlike the doctors who

"With bitter physic purge the bitter bile,"

for we rather increase and aggravate the disease. Whenever then I busy myself with such considerations as these, I try also to curtail my curiosity. For to scrutinize and pry into everything too minutely, and to overhaul every business of a servant, or action of a friend, or pastime of a son, or whisper of a wife, produces frequent, indeed daily, fits of anger, caused entirely by peevishness and harshness of character. Euripides says that the Deity

"In great things intervenes, but small things leaves
To fortune;"

but I am of opinion that a prudent man should commit nothing to fortune, nor neglect anything, but should put some things in his wife's hands to manage, others in the hands of his servants, others in the hands of his friends, (as a governor has his stewards, and financiers, and controllers), while he himself superintends the most important and weighty matters. For as small writing strains the eyes, so small matters even more strain and bother people, and stir up their anger, which carries this evil habit to greater matters. Above all I thought that saying of Empedocles, "Fast from evil," a great and divine one, and I approved of those promises and vows as not ungraceful or unphilosophical, to abstain for a year from wine and Venus, honouring the deity by continence, or for a stated time to give up lying, taking great heed to ourselves to be truthful always whether in play or earnest. With these I compared my own vow, as no less pleasing to the gods and holy, first to abstain from anger for a few days, like spending days without drunkenness or even without wine at all, offering as it were wineless offerings of honey. Then I tried for a month or two, and so in time made some progress in forbearance by earnest resolve, and by keeping myself courteous and without anger and using fair language, purifying myself from evil words and absurd actions, and from passion which for a little unlovely pleasure pays us with great mental disturbance and the bitterest repentance. In consequence of all this my experience, and the assistance of the deity, has made me form the view, that courtesy and gentleness and kindliness are not so agreeable, and pleasant, and delightful, to any of those we live with as to ourselves, that have those qualities.

Courtesy and kindliness are not so agreeable to any of those we live with as to ourselves.

On Contentedness of Mind.
Plutarch Sends Greeting to Paccius.

It was late when I received your letter, asking me to write to you something on contentedness of mind, and on those things in the Timæus that require an accurate explanation. And it so fell out that at that very time our friend Eros was obliged to set sail at once for Rome, having received a letter from the excellent Fundanus, urging haste according to his wont. And not having as much time as I could have wished to meet your request, and yet not thinking for one moment of letting my messenger go to you entirely empty-handed, I copied out the notes that I had chanced to make on contentedness of mind. For I thought that you did not desire this discourse merely to be treated to a subject handled in fine style, but for the real business of life. And I congratulate you that, though you have friendships with princes, and have as much forensic reputation as anybody, yet you are not in the same plight as the tragic Merops, nor have you like him by the felicitations of the multitude been induced to forget the sufferings of humanity; but you remember, what you have often heard, that a patrician's slipper is no cure for the gout, nor a costly ring for a whitlow, nor a diadem for the headache. For how can riches, or fame, or power at court help us to ease of mind or a calm life, unless we enjoy them when present, but are not for ever pining after them when absent? And what else causes this but the long exercise and practice of reason, which, when the unreasoning and emotional part of the soul breaks out of bounds, curbs it quickly, and does not allow it to be carried away headlong from its actual position? And as Xenophon advised that we should remember and honour the gods most especially in prosperity, that so, when we should be in any strait, we might confidently call upon them as already our well-wishers and friends; so sensible men would do well before trouble comes to meditate on remedies how to bear it, that they may be the more efficacious from being ready for use long before. For as savage dogs are excited at every sound, and are only soothed by a familiar voice, so also it is not easy to quiet the wild passions of the soul, unless familiar and well-known arguments be at hand to check its excitement.

II. He then that said, that the man that wished to have an easy mind ought to have little to do either public or private, first of all makes ease of mind a very costly article for us, if it is to be bought at the price of doing nothing, as if he should advise every sick person,

"Lie still, poor wretch, in bed."

It is false that those that have little to do are easy in mind.

And indeed stupor is a bad remedy for the body against despair, nor is he any better physician of the soul who removes its trouble and anxiety by recommending a lazy and soft life and a leaving our friends and relations and country in the lurch. In the next place, it is false that those that have little to do are easy in mind. For then women would be easier in mind than men, since they mostly stay at home in inactivity, and even now-a-days it is as Hesiod says,

On Contentedness of Mind

"The North Wind comes not near a soft-skinned maiden;"

yet griefs and troubles and unrest, proceeding from jealousy or superstition or ambition or vanity, inundate the women's part of the house with unceasing flow. And Lærtes, though he lived for twenty years a solitary life in the country,

> *"With an old woman to attend on him,*
> *Who duly set on board his meat and drink,"*

and fled from his country and house and kingdom, yet had sorrow and dejection as a perpetual companion with leisure. And some have been often thrown into sad unrest merely from inaction, as the following,

> *"But fleet Achilles, Zeus-sprung, son of Peleus,*
> *Sat by the swiftly-sailing ships and fumed,*
> *Nor ever did frequent th'ennobling council,*
> *Nor ever join the war, but pined in heart,*
> *Though in his tent abiding, for the fray."*

And full of emotion and distress at this state of things he himself says,

> *"A useless burden to the earth I sit*
> *Beside the ships."*

So even Epicurus thinks that those who are desirous of honour and glory should not rust in inglorious ease, but use their natural talents in public life for the benefit of the community at large, seeing that they are by nature so constituted that they would be more likely to be troubled and afflicted at inaction, if they did not

Even Epicurus thinks that those who are desirous of honour and glory should use their natural talents for the benefit of the community.

get what they desired. But he is absurd in that he does not urge men of ability to take part in public life, but only the restless. But we ought not to estimate ease or unrest of mind by our many or few actions, but by their fairness or foulness. For the omission of fair actions troubles and distresses us, as I have said before, quite as much as the actual doing of foul actions.

III. As for those who think that one kind of life is especially free from trouble, as some think that of farmers, others that of bachelors, others that of kings, Menander sufficiently exposes their error in the following lines:

Changes of life do not remove the sorrows and troubles of the soul.

> "Phania, I thought those rich who need not borrow,
>   Nor groan at nights, nor cry out 'Woe is me,'
>   Kicked up and down in this untoward world,
>   But sweet and gentle sleep they may enjoy."

He then goes on to remark that he saw the rich suffering the same as the poor,

> "Trouble and life are truly near akin.
>   With the luxurious or the glorious life
>   Trouble consorts, and in the life of poverty
>   Lasts with it to the end."

But just as people on the sea, timid and prone to sea-sickness, think they will suffer from it less on board a merchantman than on a boat, and for the same reason shift their quarters to a trireme, but do not attain anything by these changes, for they take with them their timidity and qualmishness, so changes of life do not remove the sorrows and troubles of the soul; which proceed from want of experience and reflection, and from inability or

ignorance rightly to enjoy the present. These afflict the rich as
well as the poor; these trouble the married as well as the
unmarried; these make people shun the forum, but find no
happiness in retirement; these make people eagerly desire
introductions at court, though when got they straightway care
no more about them.

> *"The sick are peevish in their straits and needs."*

For the wife bothers them, and they grumble at the doctor, and
they find the bed uneasy, and, as Ion says,

> *"The friend that visits them tires their patience,*
> *And yet they do not like him to depart."*

But afterwards, when the illness is over, and a sounder condition
supervenes, health returns and makes all things pleasant and
acceptable. He that yesterday loathed eggs and cakes of finest meal
and purest bread will to-day eat eagerly and with appetite coarsest
bread with a few olives and cress.

IV. Such contentedness and change of view in regard to every
kind of life does the infusion of reason bring about. When
Alexander heard from Anaxarchus of the infinite number of
worlds, he wept, and when his friends asked him what was the
matter, he replied, "Is it not a matter for tears that, when the
number of worlds is infinite, I have not conquered one?" But
Crates, who had only a wallet and threadbare cloak, passed all his
life jesting and laughing as if at a festival. Agamemnon was
troubled with his rule over so many subjects,

> *"You look on Agamemnon, Atreus' son,*

Let us cleanse therefore the fountain of contentedness, which is within us.

Those who live at random and without judgement are unduly elated by prosperity, and cast down by adversity.

Whom Zeus has plunged for ever in a mass
Of never-ending cares."

But Diogenes when he was being sold sat down and kept jeering at the auctioneer, and would not stand up when he bade him, but said joking and laughing, "Would you tell a fish you were selling to stand up?" And Socrates in prison played the philosopher and discoursed with his friends. But Phäethon, when he got up to heaven, wept because nobody gave to him his father's horses and chariot. As therefore the shoe is shaped by the foot, and not the foot by the shoe, so does the disposition make the life similar to itself. For it is not, as one said, custom that makes the best life seem sweet to those that choose it, but it is sense that makes that very life at once the best and sweetest. Let us cleanse therefore the fountain of contentedness, which is within us, that so external things may turn out for our good, through our putting the best face on them.

"Events will take their course, it is no good
Our being angry at them, he is happiest
Who wisely turns them to the best account."

V. Plato compared human life to a game at dice, wherein we ought to throw according to our requirements, and, having thrown, to make the best use of whatever turns up. It is not in our power indeed to determine what the throw will be, but it is our part, if we are wise, to accept in a right spirit whatever fortune sends, and so to contrive matters that what we wish should do us most good, and what we do not wish should do us least harm. For those who live at random and without judgement, like those sickly people who can stand neither heat nor cold, are unduly elated by prosperity, and cast down by adversity; and in either case suffer from unrest, but 'tis their own fault, and perhaps they suffer most in what are called good circumstances. Theodorus, who was surnamed the Atheist, used to say that he held out arguments with his right hand, but his hearers received them with their left; so awkward people frequently take in a clumsy manner the favours of fortune; but men of sense, as bees extract honey from thyme which is the strongest and driest of herbs, so from the least auspicious circumstances frequently derive advantage and profit.

VI. We ought then to cultivate such a habit as this, like the man who threw a stone at his dog, and missed it, but hit his step-mother, and cried out, "Not so bad." Thus we may often turn the edge of fortune when things turn not out as we wish. Diogenes was driven into exile; "not so bad;" for his exile made him turn philosopher. And Zeno of Cittium, when he heard that the only merchantman he had was wrecked, cargo and all, said, "Fortune, you treat me handsomely, since you reduce me to my threadbare cloak and piazza." What prevents our imitating such men as these? Have you failed to get some office? You will be able to live in the country henceforth, and manage your own affairs. Did you court the friendship of some great man, and meet with a rebuff? You will live free from danger and cares. Have you again had matters to deal with that required labour and thought? "Warm water will not so much make the limbs soft by soaking," to quote Pindar, as glory and honour and power make "labour sweet, and toil to be no toil." Or has any bad luck or contumely fallen on you in consequence of some calumny or from envy? The breeze is favourable that will waft you to the Muses and the Academy, as it did Plato when his friendship with Dionysius came to an end. It does indeed greatly conduce to contentedness of mind to see how famous men have borne the same troubles with an unruffled mind. For example, does childlessness trouble you? Consider

Have you failed to get some office? You will be able to live in the country henceforth, and manage your own affairs.

those kings of the Romans, none of whom left his kingdom to a son. Are you distressed at the pinch of poverty? Who of the Boeotians would you rather prefer to be than Epaminondas, or of the Romans than Fabricius? Has your wife been seduced? Have you never read that inscription at Delphi,

"Agis the king of land and sea erected me;"

and have you not heard that his wife Timæa was seduced by Alcibiades, and in her whispers to her handmaidens called the child that was born Alcibiades? Yet this did not prevent Agis from being the most famous and greatest of the Greeks. Neither again did the licentiousness of his daughter prevent Stilpo from leading the merriest life of all the philosophers that were his contemporaries. And when Metrocles reproached him with her life, he said, "Is it my fault or hers?" And when Metrocles answered, "Her fault, but your misfortune," he rejoined, "How say you? Are not faults also slips?" "Certainly," said he. "And are not slips mischances in those matters wherein we slip?" Metrocles assented. "And are not mischances misfortunes in those matters wherein we mischance?" By this gentle and philosophical argument he demonstrated the Cynic's reproach to be an idle bark.

If you take people as they are, as you would look upon barking dogs as only following their nature, you will be happier in the disposition you will then have.

VII. But most people are troubled and exasperated not only at the bad in their friends and intimates, but also in their enemies. For railing and anger and envy and malignity and jealousy and ill-will are the bane of those that suffer from those infirmities, and trouble and exasperate the foolish: as for example the quarrels of neighbours, and peevishness of acquaintances, and the want of ability in those that manage state affairs. By these things you yourself seem to me to be put out not a little, as the doctors in

On Contentedness of Mind

Sophocles, who

"With bitter physic purge the bitter bile,"

so vexed and bitter are you at people's weaknesses and infirmities,
which is not reasonable in you. Even your own private affairs are
not always managed by simple and good and suitable instruments,
so to speak, but very frequently by sharp and crooked ones. Do
not think it then either your business, or an easy matter either, to
set all these things to rights. But if you take people as they are, as
the surgeon uses his bandages and instruments for drawing teeth,
and with cheerfulness and serenity welcome all that happens, as
you would look upon barking dogs as only following their nature,
you will be happier in the disposition you will then have than you
will be distressed at other people's disagreeableness and
shortcomings. For you will forget to make a collection of
disagreeable things, which now inundate, as some hollow and low-
lying ground, your littleness of mind and weakness, which fills
itself with other people's bad points. For seeing that some of the
philosophers censure compassion to the unfortunate (on the
ground that it is good to help our neighbours, and not to give way
to sentimental sympathy in connection with them), and, what is of
more importance, do not allow those that are conscious of their
errors and bad moral disposition to be dejected and grieved at
them, but bid them cure their defects without grief at once, is it
not altogether unreasonable, look you, to allow ourselves to be
peevish and vexed, because all those who have dealings with us
and come near us are not good and clever? Let us see to it, dear
Paccius, that we do not, whether we are aware of it or not, play
a part, really looking not at the universal defects of those that
approach us, but at our own interests through our selfishness, and
not through our hatred of evil. For excessive excitement about

It is the act of a madman to distress oneself over what is lost, and not to rejoice at what is left.

things, and an undue appetite and desire for them, or on the other hand aversion and dislike to them, engender suspiciousness and peevishness against persons, who were, we think, the cause of our being deprived of some things, and of being troubled with others. But he that is accustomed to adapt himself to things easily and calmly is most cheerful and gentle in his dealings with people.

VIII. Wherefore let us resume our argument. As in a fever everything seems bitter and unpleasant to the taste, but when we see others not loathing but fancying the very same eatables and drinkables, we no longer find the fault to be in them but in ourselves and our disease, so we shall cease to blame and be discontented with the state of affairs, if we see others cheerfully and without grief enduring the same. It also makes for contentedness, when things happen against our wish, not to overlook our many advantages and comforts, but by looking at both good and bad to feel that the good preponderate. When our eyes are dazzled with things too bright we turn them away, and ease them by looking at flowers or grass, while we keep the eyes of our mind strained on disagreeable things, and force them to dwell on bitter ideas, well-nigh tearing them away by force from the consideration of pleasanter things. And yet one might apply here, not unaptly, what was said to the man of curiosity,

Suppose someone should say, What blessings have we? I would reply, What have we not?

> "Malignant wretch, why art so keen to mark
> Thy neighbour's fault, and seest not thine own?"

Why on earth, my good sir, do you confine your view to your troubles, making them so vivid and acute, while you do not let your mind dwell at all on your present comforts? But as cupping-glasses draw the worst blood from the flesh, so you force upon your attention the worst things in your lot: acting not a whit more wisely than that Chian, who, selling much choice wine to others, asked for some sour wine for his own supper; and one of his slaves being asked by another, what he had left his master doing, replied, "Asking for bad when good was by." For most people overlook the advantages and pleasures of their individual lives, and run to their difficulties and grievances. Aristippus, however, was not such a one, for he cleverly knew as in a scale to make the better preponderate over the worse. So having lost a good farm, he asked one of those who made a great show of condolence and sympathy, "Have you not only one little piece of ground, while I have three fields left?" And when he admitted that it was so, he went on to say, "Ought I not then to condole with you rather than you with me?" For it is the act of a madman to distress oneself over what is lost, and not to rejoice at what is left; but like little children, if one of their many playthings be taken away by anyone, throw the rest away and weep and cry out, so we, if we are assailed by fortune in some one point, wail and mourn and make all other things seem unprofitable in our eyes.

IX. Suppose someone should say, What blessings have we? I would reply, What have we not? One has reputation, another a house, another a wife, another a good friend. When Antipater of Tarsus was reckoning up on his death-bed his various pieces of good fortune, he did not even pass over his favourable voyage from Cilicia to Athens. So we should not overlook, but take account of everyday blessings, and rejoice that we live, and are well, and see the sun, and that no war or sedition plagues our country, but that the earth is open to cultivation, the sea secure to mariners, and that we can speak or be silent, lead a busy or an idle life, as we choose. We shall get more contentedness from the presence of all these blessings, if we fancy them as absent, and remember from time to time how people ill yearn for health, and

We shall get more contentedness from these blessings, if we remember from time to time how people ill yearn for health, and people in war for peace.

It makes much for contentedness of mind to look to our own condition, and not to compare ourselves with those who are better off.

people in war for peace, and strangers and unknown in a great city for reputation and friends, and how painful it is to be deprived of all these when one has once had them. For then each of these blessings will not appear to us only great and valuable when it is lost, and of no value while we have it. For not having it cannot add value to anything. Nor ought we to amass things we regard as valuable, and always be on the tremble and afraid of losing them as valuable things, and yet, when we have them, ignore them and think little of them; but we ought to use them for our pleasure and enjoyment, that we may bear their loss, if that should happen, with more equanimity. But most people, as Arcesilaus said, think it right to inspect minutely and in every detail, perusing them alike with the eyes of the body and mind, other people's poems and paintings and statues, while they neglect to study their own lives, which have often many not unpleasing subjects for contemplation, looking abroad and ever admiring other people's reputations and fortunes, as adulterers admire other men's wives, and think cheap of their own.

X. And yet it makes much for contentedness of mind to look for the most part at home and to our own condition, or if not, to look at the case of people worse off than ourselves, and not, as most people do, to compare ourselves with those who are better off. For example, those who are in chains think those happy who are freed from their chains, and they again freemen, and freemen citizens, and they again the rich, and the rich satraps, and satraps kings, and kings the gods, content with hardly anything short of hurling thunderbolts and lightning. And so they ever want something above them, and are never thankful for what they have.

"I care not for the wealth of golden Gyges,"

and,

> *"I never had or envy or desire*
> *To be a god, or love for mighty empire,*
> *Far distant from my eyes are all such things."*

But this, you will say, was the language of a Thasian. But you will
find others, Chians or Galatians or Bithynians, not content with
the share of glory or power they have among their fellow-citizens,
but weeping because they do not wear senators' shoes; or, if they
have them, that they cannot be prætors at Rome; or, if they get
that office, that they are not consuls; or, if they are consuls, that
they are only proclaimed second and not first. What is all this but
seeking out excuses for being unthankful to fortune, only to
torment and punish oneself? But he that has a mind in sound
condition, does not sit down in sorrow and dejection if he is less
renowned or rich than some of the countless myriads of mankind
that the sun looks upon, "who feed on the produce of the wide
world," but goes on his way rejoicing at his fortune and life, as far
fairer and happier than that of myriads of others. In the Olympian
games it is not possible to be the victor by choosing one's
competitors. But in the race of life circumstances allow us to
plume ourselves on surpassing many, and to be objects of envy
rather than to have to envy others, unless we pit ourselves against
a Briareus or a Hercules. Whenever then you admire anyone
carried by in his litter as a greater man than yourself, lower your
eyes and look at those that bear the litter. And when you think the
famous Xerxes happy for his passage over the Hellespont, as a
native of those parts did, look too at those who dug through
Mount Athos under the lash, and at those whose ears and noses
were cut off because the bridge was broken by the waves, consider
their state of mind also, for they think your life and fortunes

Open and draw the gaudy curtain of their pomp and show, and you will see that they have much to trouble them.

happy. Socrates, when he heard one of his friends saying, "How dear this city is! Chian wine costs one mina, a purple robe three, and half a pint of honey five drachmæ," took him to the meal market, and showed him half a peck of meal for an obol, then took him to the olive market, and showed him a peck of olives for two coppers, and lastly showed him that a sleeveless vest was only ten drachmæ. At each place Socrates' friend exclaimed, "How cheap this city is!" So also we, when we hear anyone saying that our affairs are bad and in a woful plight, because we are not consuls or governors, may reply, "Our affairs are in an admirable condition, and our life an enviable one, seeing that we do not beg, nor carry burdens, nor live by flattery."

XI. But since through our folly we are accustomed to live more with an eye to others than ourselves, and since nature is so jealous and envious that it rejoices not so much in its own blessings as it is pained by those of others, do not look only at the much-cried-up splendour of those whom you envy and admire, but open and draw, as it were, the gaudy curtain of their pomp and show, and peep within, you will see that they have much to trouble them, and many things to annoy them. The well-known Pittacus, whose fame was so great for fortitude and wisdom and uprightness, was once entertaining some guests, and his wife came in in a rage and upset the table, and as the guests were dismayed he said, Every one of you has some trouble, and he who has mine only is not so bad off.

Self-love is mainly to blame, making people fond of being first and insatiably desirous to engage in everything.

> "Happy is he accounted at the forum,
> But when he opens the door of his own house
> Thrice miserable; for his wife rules all,
> Still lords it over him, and is ever quarrelling.
> Many griefs has he that I wot not of."

Many such cases are there, unknown to the public, for family pride casts a veil over them, to be found in wealth and glory and even in royalty.

> *"O happy son of Atreus, child of destiny,*
> *Blessed thy lot;"*

congratulation like this comes from an external view, from a halo of arms and horses and the pomp of war, but the inward voice of emotion testifies against all this vain glory;

> *"A heavy fate is laid on me by Zeus*
> *The son of Cronos."*

And,

> *"Old man, I think your lot one to be envied,*
> *As that of any man who free from danger*
> *Passes his life unknown and in obscurity."*

By such reflections as these one may wean oneself from that discontent with one's fortune, which makes one's own condition look low and mean from too much admiring one's neighbour's.

XII. Another thing, which is a great hindrance to peace of mind, is not to proportion our desires to our means, but to carry too much sail, as it were, in our hopes of great things and then, if unsuccessful, to blame destiny and fortune, and not our own folly. For he is not unfortunate who wishes to shoot with a plough, or hunt the hare with an ox; nor has he an evil genius opposed to him, who does not catch deer with fishing nets, but merely is the dupe of his own stupidity and folly in attempting impossibilities.

So that all things are not within any one's power, we must adapt ourselves to our natural bent, and not drag and force nature to some other kind of life.

119

Self-love is mainly to blame, making people fond of being first and aspiring in all matters, and insatiably desirous to engage in everything. For people not only wish at one and the same time to be rich, and learned, and strong, and boon-companions, and agreeable, and friends of kings, and governors of cities, but they are also discontented if they have not dogs and horses and quails and cocks of the first quality. Dionysius the elder was not content with being the most powerful monarch of his times, but because he could not beat Philoxenus the poet in singing, or surpass Plato in dialectics, was so angry and exasperated that he put the one to work in his stone quarries, and sent the other to Ægina and sold him there. Alexander was of a different spirit, for when Crisso the famous runner ran a race with him, and seemed to let the king outrun him on purpose, he was greatly displeased. Good also was the spirit of Achilles in Homer, who, when he said,

> *"None of the Achæan warriors is a match*
> *For me in war,"*

added,

> *"Yet in the council hall*
> *Others there are who better are than me."*

And when Megabyzus the Persian visited the studio of Apelles, and began to chatter about art, Apelles stopped him and said, "While you kept silence you seemed to be somebody from your gold and purple, but now these lads that are grinding colours are laughing at your nonsense." But some who think the Stoics only talk idly, in styling their wise man not only prudent and just and brave but also orator and general and poet and rich man and king, yet claim for themselves all those titles, and are indignant if they

Runners are not discontented because they do not carry off the crowns of wrestlers, but rejoice and delight in their own crowns.

do not get them. And yet even among the gods different functions are assigned to different personages; thus one is called the god of war, another the god of oracles, another the god of gain, and Aphrodite, as she has nothing to do with warlike affairs, is despatched by Zeus to marriages and bridals.

XIII. And indeed there are some pursuits which cannot exist together, but are by their very nature opposed. For example oratory and the study of the mathematics require ease and leisure; whereas political ability and the friendship of kings cannot be attained without mixing in affairs and in public life. Moreover wine and indulgence in meat make the body indeed strong and vigorous, but blunt the intellect; and though unremitting attention to making and saving money will heap up wealth, yet despising and contemning riches is a great help to philosophy. So that all things are not within any one's power, and we must obey that saying inscribed in the temple of Apollo at Delphi, *Know thyself,* and adapt ourselves to our natural bent, and not drag and force nature to some other kind of life or pursuit. "The horse to the chariot, and the ox to the plough, and swiftly alongside the ship scuds the dolphin, while he that meditates destruction for the boar must find a staunch hound." But he that chafes and is grieved that he is not at one and the same time "a lion reared on the mountains, exulting in his strength," and a little Maltese lap-dog reared in the lap of a rich widow, is out of his senses. And not a whit wiser is he who wishes to be an Empedocles, or Plato, or Democritus, and write about the world and the real nature of things, and at the same time to be married like Euphorion to a rich wife, or to revel and drink with Alexander like Medius; and is grieved and vexed if he is not also admired for his wealth like Ismenias, and for his virtue like Epaminondas. But runners are not discontented because they do not carry off the crowns of

Those that think so highly of their own walk in life will not be so envious about their neighbours'.

We ought each therefore to select the calling appropriate for ourselves and labour energetically in it.

wrestlers, but rejoice and delight in their own crowns. "You are a citizen of Sparta: see you make the most of her." So too said Solon:

> *"We will not change our virtue for their wealth,*
> *For virtue never dies, but wealth has wings,*
> *And flies about from one man to another."*

And Strato the natural philosopher, when he heard that Menedemus had many more pupils than he had, said, "Is it wonderful at all that more wish to wash than to be anointed?" And Aristotle, writing to Antipater, said, "Not only has Alexander a right to plume himself on his rule over many subjects, but no less legitimate is satisfaction at entertaining right opinions about the gods." For those that think so highly of their own walk in life will not be so envious about their neighbours'. We do not expect a vine to bear figs, nor an olive grapes, yet now-a-days, with regard to ourselves, if we have not at one and the same time the privilege of being accounted rich and learned, generals and philosophers, flatterers and outspoken, stingy and extravagant, we slander ourselves and are dissatisfied, and despise ourselves as living a maimed and imperfect life. Furthermore, we see that nature teaches us the same lesson. For as she provides different kinds of beasts with different kinds of food, and has not made all carnivorous, or seed-pickers, or root-diggers, so she has given to mankind various means of getting a livelihood, "one by keeping sheep, another by ploughing, another by fowling," and another by catching the fish of the sea. We ought each therefore to select the calling appropriate for ourselves and labour energetically in it, and leave other people to theirs, and not demonstrate Hesiod as coming short of the real state of things when he said,

On Contentedness of Mind

"Potter is wroth with potter, smith with smith."

For not only do people envy those of the same trade and manner of life, but the rich envy the learned, and the famous the rich, and advocates sophists, aye, and freemen and patricians admire and think happy comedians starring it at the theatres, and dancers, and the attendants at kings' courts, and by all this envy give themselves no small trouble and annoyance.

XIV. But that every man has in himself the magazines of content or discontent, and that the jars containing blessings and evils are not on the threshold of Zeus, but lie stored in the mind, is plain from the differences of men's passions. For the foolish overlook and neglect present blessings, through their thoughts being ever intent on the future; but the wise make the past clearly present to them through memory. For the present giving only a moment of time to the touch, and then evading our grasp, does not seem to the foolish to be ours or to belong to us at all. And like that person painted as rope-making in Hades and permitting an ass feeding by to eat up the rope as fast as he makes it, so the stupid and thankless forgetfulness of most people comes upon them and takes possession of them, and obliterates from their mind every past action, whether success, or pleasant leisure, or society, or enjoyment, and breaks the unity of life which arises from the past being blended with the present; for detaching to-day from both yesterday and to-morrow, it soon makes every event as if it had never happened from lack of memory. For as those in the schools, who deny the growth of our bodies by reason of the continual flux of substance, make each of us in theory different from himself and another man, so those who do not keep or recall to their memory former things, but let them drift, actually empty themselves daily, and hang upon the morrow, as if what happened

The wise make the past clearly present to them through memory.

a year ago, or even yesterday and the day before yesterday, had nothing to do with them, and had hardly occurred at all.

XV. This is one great hindrance to contentedness of mind, and another still greater is whenever, like flies that slide down smooth places in mirrors, but stick fast in rough places or where there are cracks, men let pleasant and agreeable things glide from their memory, and pin themselves down to the remembrance of unpleasant things; or rather, as at Olynthus they say beetles, when they get into a certain place called Destruction-to-beetles, cannot get out, but fly round and round till they die, so men will glide into the remembrance of their woes, and will not give themselves a respite from sorrow. But, as we use our brightest colours in a picture, so in the mind we ought to look at the cheerful and bright side of things, and hide and keep down the gloomy, for we cannot altogether obliterate or get rid of it. For, as the strings of the bow and lyre are alternately tightened and relaxed, so is it with the order of the world; in human affairs there is nothing pure and without alloy. But as in music there are high and low notes, and in grammar vowels and mutes, but neither the musician nor grammarian decline to use either kinds, but know how to blend and employ them both for their purpose, so in human affairs which are balanced one against another,—for, as Euripides says,

> *"There is no good without ill in the world,*
> *But everything is mixed in due proportion,"—*

we ought not to be disheartened or despondent; but as musicians drown their worst music with the best, so should we take good and bad together, and make our chequered life one of convenience and harmony. For it is not, as Menander says,

As the strings of the lyre are alternately tightened and relaxed, so is it with the order of the world; in human affairs there is nothing without alloy.

"Directly any man is born, a genius
Befriends him, a good guide to him for life,"

but it is rather, as Empedocles states, two fates or genii take hold of each of us when we are born and govern us. "There were Chthonia and far-seeing Heliope, and cruel Deris, and grave Harmonia, and Callisto, and Æschra, and Thoosa, and Denæa, and charming Nemertes, and Asaphea with the black fruit."

XVI. And as at our birth we received the mingled seeds of each of these passions, which is the cause of much irregularity, the sensible person hopes for better things, but expects worse, and makes the most of either, remembering that wise maxim, *Not too much of anything.* For not only will he who is least solicitous about to-morrow best enjoy it when it comes, as Epicurus says, but also wealth, and renown, and power and rule, gladden most of all the hearts of those who are least afraid of the contrary. For the immoderate desire for each, implanting a most immoderate fear of losing them, makes the enjoyment of them weak and wavering, like a flame under the influence of a wind. But he whom reason enables to say to fortune without fear or trembling,

"If you bring any good I gladly welcome it,
But if you fail me little does it trouble me,"

he can enjoy the present with most zest through his confidence, and absence of fear of the loss of what he has, which would be unbearable. For we may not only admire but also imitate the behaviour of Anaxagoras, which made him cry out at the death of his son, "I knew I had begot a mortal," and apply it to every contingency. For example, "I know that wealth is ephemeral and insecure; I know that those who gave power can take it away again;

The sensible person hopes for better things, but expects worse, and makes the most of either.

I know that my wife is good, but still a woman; and that my friend, since a human being, is by nature a changeable animal, to use Plato's expression." For such a prepared frame of mind, if anything happens unwished for but not unexpected, not admitting of such phrases as "I shouldn't have dreamed of it," or "I expected quite a different lot," or "I didn't look for this," abates the violent beatings and palpitations of the heart, and quickly causes wild unrest to subside. Carneades indeed reminds us that in great matters the unexpected makes the sum total of grief and dejection. Certainly the kingdom of Macedonia was many times smaller than the Roman Empire, but when Perseus lost Macedonia, he not only himself bewailed his wretched fate, but seemed to all men the most unfortunate and unlucky of mankind; yet Æmilius who conquered him, though he had to give up to another the command both by land and sea, yet was crowned, and offered sacrifice, and was justly esteemed happy. For he knew that he had taken a command which he would have to give up, but Perseus lost his kingdom without expecting it. Well also has the poet shown the power of anything that happens unexpectedly. For Odysseus wept bitterly at the death of his dog, but was not so moved when he sat by his wife who wept, for in the latter case he had come fully determined to keep his emotion under the control of reason, whereas in the former it was against his expectation, and therefore fell upon him as a sudden blow.

XVII. And since generally speaking some things which happen against our will pain and trouble us by their very nature, while in the case of most we accustom ourselves and learn to be disgusted with them from fancy, it is not unprofitable to counteract this to have ever ready that line of Menander,

"You suffer no dread thing but in your fancy."

Fortune can take away our money, but cannot make a high-souled man bad and cowardly.

For what, if they touch you neither in soul nor body, are such things to you as the low birth of your father, or the adultery of your wife, or the loss of some prize or precedence, since even by their absence a man is not prevented from being in excellent condition both of body and soul. And with respect to the things that seem to pain us by their very nature, as sickness, and anxieties, and the deaths of friends and children, we should remember that line of Euripides,

> *"Alas! and why alas? we only suffer*
> *What mortals must expect."*

For no argument has so much weight with emotion when it is borne down with grief, as that which reminds it of the common and natural necessity to which man is exposed owing to the body, the only handle which he gives to fortune, for in his most important and influential part he is secure against external things. When Demetrius captured Megara, he asked Stilpo if any of his things had been plundered, and Stilpo answered, "I saw nobody carrying off anything of mine." And so when fortune has plundered us and stripped us of everything else, we have that within ourselves

> *"Which the Achæans ne'er could rob us of."*

So that we ought not altogether to abase and lower nature, as if she had no strength or stability against fortune; but on the contrary, knowing that the rotten and perishable part of man, wherein alone he lies open to fortune, is small, while we ourselves are masters of the better part, wherein are situated our greatest blessings, as good opinions and teaching and virtuous precepts, all which things cannot be abstracted from us or perish, we ought to

He who understands the nature of the soul has in his fearlessness of death no small help to ease of mind in life.

We ought to try and test ourselves in smaller matters with a view to greater.

look on the future with invincible courage, and say to fortune, as Socrates is supposed to have said to his accusers Anytus and Melitus before the jury, "Anytus and Melitus can kill me, but they cannot hurt me." For fortune can afflict us with disease, take away our money, calumniate us to the people or king, but cannot make a good and brave and high-souled man bad and cowardly and low and ignoble and envious, nor take away that disposition of mind, whose constant presence is of more use for the conduct of life than the presence of a pilot at sea. For the pilot cannot make calm the wild wave or wind, nor can he find a haven at his need wherever he wishes, nor can he await his fate with confidence and without trembling, but as long as he has not despaired, but uses his skill, he scuds before the gale, "lowering his big sail, till his lower mast is only just above the sea dark as Erebus," and sits at the helm trembling and quaking. But the disposition of a wise man gives calm even to the body, mostly cutting off the causes of diseases by temperance and plain living and moderate exercise; but if some beginning of trouble arise from without, as we avoid a sunken rock, so he passes by it with furled sail, as Asclepiades puts it; but if some unexpected and tremendous gale come upon him and prove too much for him, the harbour is at hand, and he can swim away from the body, as from a leaky boat.

XVIII. For it is the fear of death, and not the desire of life, that makes the foolish person to hang to the body, clinging to it, as Odysseus did to the fig-tree from fear of Charybdis that lay below,

"Where the wind neither let him stay, or sail,"

so that he was displeased at this, and afraid of that. But he who understands somehow or other the nature of the soul, and reflects that the change it will undergo at death will be either to something better or at least not worse, he has in his fearlessness of death no small help to ease of mind in life. For to one who can enjoy life when virtue and what is congenial to him have the upper hand, and that can fearlessly depart from life, when uncongenial and unnatural things are in the ascendant, with the words on his lips,

"The deity shall free me, when I will,"

what can we imagine could befall such a man as this that would vex him and wear him and harass him? For he who said, "I have anticipated you, O fortune, and cut off all your loopholes to get at me," did not trust to bolts or keys or walls, but to determination and reason, which are within the power of all persons that choose. And we ought not to despair or disbelieve any of these sayings, but admiring them and emulating them and being enthusiastic about them, we ought to try and test ourselves in smaller matters with a view to greater, not avoiding or rejecting that self-examination, nor sheltering ourselves under the remark, "Perhaps nothing will be more difficult." For inertia and softness are generated by that self-indulgence which ever occupies itself only with the easiest tasks, and flees from the disagreeable to what is most pleasant. But the soul that accustoms itself to face steadily sickness and grief and exile, and calls in reason to its help in each case, will find in what appears so sore and dreadful much that is false, empty, and rotten, as reason will show in each case.

In the mind of the wise man good actions always leave a fresh and fragrant memory.

XIX. And yet many shudder at that line of Menander,

"No one can say, I shall not suffer this or that,"

being ignorant how much it helps us to freedom from grief to practise to be able to look fortune in the face with our eyes open, and not to entertain fine and soft fancies, like one reared in the shade on many hopes that always yield and never resist. We can, however, answer Menander's line,

"No one can say, I shall not suffer this or that,"

for a man can say, "I will not do this or that, I will not lie, I will not play the rogue, I will not cheat, I will not scheme." For this is in our power, and is no small but great help to ease of mind. As on the contrary

"The consciousness of having done ill deeds,"

like a sore in the flesh, leaves in the mind a regret which ever wounds it and pricks it. For reason banishes all other griefs, but itself creates regret when the soul is vexed with shame and self-tormented. For as those who shudder in ague-fits or burn in fevers feel more trouble and distress than those who externally suffer the same from cold or heat, so the grief is lighter which comes externally from chance, but that lament,

"None is to blame for this but I myself,"

"Does not a good man consider every day a feast?"

coming from within on one's own misdeeds, intensifies one's bitterness by the shame felt. And so neither costly house, nor quantity of gold, nor pride of race, nor weighty office, nor grace of language, nor eloquence, impart so much calm and serenity to life, as a soul pure from evil acts and desires, having an imperturbable and undefiled character as the source of its life; whence good actions flow, producing an enthusiastic and cheerful energy accompanied by loftiness of thought, and a memory sweeter and more lasting than that hope which Pindar says is the support of old age. Censers do not, as Carneades said, after they are emptied, long retain their sweet smell; but in the mind of the wise man good actions always leave a fresh and fragrant memory, by which joy is watered and flourishes, and despises those who wail over life and abuse it as a region of ills, or as a place of exile for souls in this world.

XX. I am very taken with Diogenes' remark to a stranger at Lacedæmon, who was dressing with much display for a feast, "Does not a good man consider every day a feast?" And a very great feast too, if we live soberly. For the world is a most holy and divine temple, into which man is introduced at his birth, not to behold motionless images made by hands, but those things (to use the language of Plato) which the divine mind has exhibited as the visible representations of invisible things, having innate in them the principle of life and motion, as the sun moon and stars, and rivers ever flowing with fresh water, and the earth affording maintenance to plants and animals. Seeing then that life is the most complete initiation into all these things, it ought to be full of ease of mind and joy; not as most people wait for the festivals of Cronos and Dionysus and the Panathenæa and other similar days, that they may joy and refresh themselves with bought laughter, paying actors and dancers for the same. On such occasions indeed we sit silently and decorously, for no one wails when he is initiated, or groans when he beholds the Pythian games, or when he is drinking at the festival of Cronos: but men shame the festivals which the deity supplies us with and initiates us in, passing most of their time in lamentation and heaviness of heart and distressing anxiety. And though men delight in the pleasing notes of musical instruments, and in the songs of birds, and behold with joy the animals playing and frisking, and on the contrary are distressed when they roar and howl and look savage; yet in regard to their own life, when they see

Remember the past with thankfulness, and meet the future without fear.

it without smiles and dejected, and ever oppressed and afflicted by the most wretched sorrows and toils and unending cares, they do not think of trying to procure alleviation and ease. How is this? Nay, they will not even listen to others' exhortation, which would enable them to acquiesce in the present without repining, and to remember the past with thankfulness, and to meet the future hopefully and cheerfully without fear or suspicion.

How One Can Praise Oneself Without Exciting Envy.

To speak to other people about one's own importance or ability, Herculanus, is universally declared to be tiresome and illiberal, but in fact not many even of those who censure it avoid its unpleasantness. Thus Euripides, though he says,

"If words had to be bought by human beings,
No one would wish to trumpet his own praises.
But since one can get words sans any payment
From lofty ether, everyone delights
In speaking truth or falsehood of himself,
For he can do it with impunity;"

yet uses much tiresome boasting, intermixing with the passion and action of his plays irrelevant matter about himself. Similarly Pindar says, that "to boast unseasonably is to play an accompaniment to madness," yet he does not cease to talk big about his own merit, which indeed is well worthy of encomium, who would deny it? But those who are crowned in the games leave it to others to celebrate their victories, to avoid the unpleasantness of singing their own praises. So we are with justice disgusted at Timotheus for trumpeting his own glory inelegantly and contrary

to custom in the inscription for his victory over Phrynis, "A proud day for you, Timotheus, was it when the herald cried out, 'The Milesian Timotheus is victorious over the son of Carbo and his Ionic notes.'" As Xenophon says, "Praise from others is the pleasantest thing a man can hear," but to others a man's self-praise is most nauseous. For first we think those impudent who praise themselves, since modesty would be becoming even if they were praised by others; secondly, we think them unjust in giving themselves what they ought to receive from others; thirdly, if we are silent we seem to be vexed and to envy them, and if we are afraid of this imputation, we are obliged to heap praise upon them contrary to our real opinion, and to bear them out, undertaking a task more befitting gross flattery than honour.

II. And yet, in spite of all this, there are occasions when a statesman may venture to speak in his own praise, not to cry up his own glory and merit, but when the time and matter demand that he should speak the truth about himself, as he would about another; especially when it is mentioned that another has done good and excellent things, there is no need for him to suppress the fact that he has done as well. For such self-praise bears excellent fruit, since much more and better praise springs from it as from seed. For the statesman does not ask for reputation as a reward or consolation, nor is he merely pleased at its attending upon his actions, but he values it because credit and character give him opportunities to do good on a larger scale. For it is both easy and pleasant to benefit those who believe in us and are friendly to us, but it is not easy to act virtuously against suspicion and calumny, and to force one's benefits on those that reject them. Let us now consider, if there are any other reasons warranting self-praise in a statesman, what they are, that, while we avoid vain glory and disgusting other people, we may not omit any useful kind of self-praise.

The statesman does not ask for reputation as a reward or consolation, but he values it because credit and character give him opportunities to do good on a larger scale.

III. That is vain glory then when men seem to praise themselves that they may call forth the laudation of others; and it is especially despised because it seems to proceed from ambition and an unseasonable opinion of oneself. For as those who cannot obtain food are forced to feed on their own flesh against nature, and that is the end of famine, so those that hunger after praise, if they get no one else to praise them, disgrace themselves by their anxiety to feed their own vanity. But when, not merely content with praising themselves, they vie with the praise of others, and pit their own deeds and actions against theirs, with the intent of outshining them, they add envy and malignity to their vanity. The proverb teaches us that to put our foot into another's dance is meddlesome and ridiculous; we ought equally to be on our guard against intruding our own panegyric into others' praises out of envy and spite, nor should we allow others either to praise us then, but we should make way for those that are being honoured, if they are worthy of honour, and even if they seem to us undeserving of honour and worthless, we ought not to strip them of their praise by self-laudation, but by direct argument and proof that they are not worthy of all these encomiums. It is plain then that we ought to avoid all such conduct as this.

IV. But self-praise cannot be blamed, if it is an answer to some charge or calumny, as those words of Pericles, "And yet you are angry with such a man as me, a man I take it inferior to no one either in knowledge of what should be done, or in ability to point out the same, and a lover of my country to boot, and superior to bribes." For not only did he avoid all swagger and vainglory and ambition in talking thus loftily about himself, but he also exhibited the spirit and greatness of his virtue, which could abase and crush envy because it could not be abased itself. For people will hardly condemn such men, for they are elevated and cheered

Those that hunger after praise disgrace themselves by their anxiety to feed their own vanity.

Notice in his speech that he most artistically inserts praise of his audience in the remarks about himself, and so makes his speech less egotistical and less likely to raise envy....

and inspired by noble self-laudation such as this, if it have a true basis, as all history testifies. Thus the Thebans, when their generals were charged with not returning home, and laying down their office of Boeotarchs when their time had expired, but instead of that making inroads into Laconia, and helping Messene, hardly acquitted Pelopidas, who was submissive and suppliant, but for Epaminondas, who gloried in what he had done, and at last said that he was ready to die, if they would confess that he had ravaged Laconia, and restored Messene, and made Arcadia one state, against the will of the Thebans, they would not pass sentence upon him, but admired his heroism, and with rejoicing and smiles set him free. So too we must not altogether find fault with Sthenelus in Homer saying,

"We boast ourselves far better than our fathers,"

when we remember the words of Agamemnon,

*"How now? thou son of brave horse-taming Tydeus,
Why dost thou crouch for fear, and watch far off
The lines of battle? How unlike thy father!"*

For it was not because he was defamed himself, but he stood up for his friend that was abused, the occasion giving him a reasonable excuse for self-commendation. So too the Romans were far from pleased at Cicero's frequently passing encomiums upon himself in the affair of Catiline, yet when Scipio said they ought not to try him (Scipio), since he had given them the power to try anybody, they put on garlands, and accompanied him to the Capitol, and sacrificed with him. For Cicero was not compelled to praise himself, but only did so for glory, whereas the danger in which Scipio stood removed envy from him.

On Contentedness of Mind

V. And not only on one's trial and in danger, but also in misfortune, is tall talk and boasting more suitable than in prosperity. For in prosperity people seem to clutch as it were at glory and enjoy it, and so gratify their ambition; but in adversity, being far from ambition owing to circumstances, such self-commendation seems to be a bearing up and fortifying the spirit against fortune, and an avoidance altogether of that desire for pity and condolence, and that humility, which we often find in adversity. As then we esteem those persons vain and without sense who in walking hold themselves very erect and with a stiff neck, yet in boxing or fighting we commend such as hold themselves up and alert, so the man struggling with adversity, who stands up straight against his fate, "in fighting posture like some boxer," and instead of being humble and abject becomes through his boasting lofty and dignified, seems to be not offensive and impudent, but great and invincible. This is why, I suppose, Homer has represented Patroclus modest and without reproach in prosperity, yet at the moment of death saying grandiloquently,

...for they rejoice at the enumeration of their successes.

> *"Had twenty warriors fought me such as thou,*
> *All had succumbed to my victorious spear."*

And Phocion, though in other respects he was gentle, yet after his sentence exhibited his greatness of soul to many others, and notably to one of those that were to die with him, who was weeping and wailing, to whom he said, "What! are you not content to die with Phocion?"

VI. Not less, but still more, lawful is it for a public man who is wronged to speak on his own behalf to those who treat him with ingratitude. Thus Achilles generally conceded glory to the gods, and modestly used such language as,

> *"If ever Zeus*
> *Shall grant to me to sack Troy's well-built town;"*

but when insulted and outraged contrary to his deserts, he utters in his rage boastful words,

> *"Alighting from my ships twelve towns I sacked,"*

and,

> *"For they will never dare to face my helmet*
> *When it gleams near."*

For frank outspokenness, when it is part of one's defence, admits of boasting. It was in this spirit no doubt that Themistocles, who neither in word nor deed had given any offence, when he saw the Athenians were tired of him and treating him with neglect, did not abstain from saying, "My good sirs, why do you tire of receiving benefits so frequently at the same hands?" and "When the storm is on you fly to me for shelter as to a tree, but when fine weather comes again, then you pass by and strip me of my leaves."

Dionysius was not aware that through his envy he was weakening the importance and dignity of his own authority.

VII. They then that are wronged generally mention what they have done well to those who are ungrateful. And the person who is blamed for what he has done well is altogether to be pardoned, and not censured, if he passes encomiums on his own actions: for he is in the position of one not scolding but making his defence. This it was that made Demosthenes' freedom of speech splendid, and prevented people being wearied out by the praise which in all his speech *On the Crown* he lavished on himself, pluming himself on those embassies and decrees in connection with the war with which fault had been found.

138

VIII. Not very unlike this is the grace of antithesis, when a person shows that the opposite of what he is charged with is base and low. Thus Lycurgus when he was charged at Athens with having bribed an informer to silence, replied, "What kind of a citizen do you think me, who, having had so long time the fingering of your public money, am detected in giving rather than taking unjustly?" And Cicero, when Metellus told him that he had destroyed more as a witness than he had got acquitted as an advocate, answered, "Who denies that my honesty is greater than my eloquence?" Compare such sayings of Demosthenes as, "Who would not have been justified in killing me, had I tried in word only to impair the ancient glory of our city?" And, "What think you these wretches would have said, if the states had departed, when I was curiously discussing these points?" And indeed the whole of that speech *On the Crown* most ingeniously introduces his own praises in his antitheses, and answers to the charges brought against him.

Men would rather ascribe their defeat to fortune than the enemy's valour, for in the former case they consider it an accident, whereas in the latter case they would have to blame themselves.

IX. However it is worth while to notice in his speech that he most artistically inserts praise of his audience in the remarks about himself, and so makes his speech less egotistical and less likely to raise envy. Thus he shows how the Athenians behaved to the Euboeans and to the Thebans, and what benefits they conferred on the people of Byzantium and on the Chersonese, claiming for himself only a subordinate part in the matter. Thus he cunningly insinuates into the audience with his own praises what they will gladly hear, for they rejoice at the enumeration of their successes, and their joy is succeeded by admiration and esteem for the person to whom the success was due. So also Epaminondas, when Meneclidas once jeered at him as thinking more of himself than Agamemnon ever did, replied, "It is your fault then, men of Thebes, by whose help alone I put down the power of the Lacedæmonians in one day."

If anyone should praise you as learned, or rich, or influential, it would be well to bid him not talk about you in that strain, but say that you were good and harmless and useful.

X. But since most people very much dislike and object to a man's praising himself, but if he praises some one else are on the contrary often glad and readily bear him out, some are in the habit of praising in season those that have the same pursuits, business and characters as themselves, and so conciliate and move the audience in their own favour; for the audience know at the moment such a one is speaking that, though he is speaking about another, yet his own similar virtue is worthy of their praise. For as one who throws in another's teeth things of which he is guilty himself must know that he upbraids himself most, so the good in paying honour to the good remind those who know their character of themselves, so that their hearers cry out at once, "Are not you such a one yourself?" Thus Alexander honouring Hercules, and Androcottus again honouring Alexander, got themselves honoured on the same grounds. Dionysius on the contrary pulling Gelon to pieces, and calling him the Gelos of Sicily, was not aware that through his envy he was weakening the importance and dignity of his own authority.

XI. These things then a public man must generally know and observe. But those that are compelled to praise themselves do so less offensively if they do not ascribe all the honour to themselves, but, being aware that their glory will be tiresome to others, set it down partly to fortune, partly to the deity. So Achilles said well,

"Since the gods granted us to kill this hero."

Well also did Timoleon, who erected a temple at Syracuse to the goddess of Fortune after his success, and dedicated his house to the Good Genius. Excellently again did Pytho of Ænos, (when he came to Athens after killing Cotys, and when the demagogues vied with one another in praising him to the people, and he observed that some were jealous and displeased,) in coming forward and saying, "Men of Athens, this is the doing of one of the gods, I only put my hands to the work." Sulla also forestalled envy by ever praising fortune, and eventually he proclaimed himself as under the protection of Aphrodite. For men would rather ascribe their defeat to fortune than the enemy's valour, for in the former case they consider it an accident, whereas in the latter case they would have to blame themselves and set it down to their own shortcomings. So they say the legislation of Zaleucus pleased the Locrians not least, because he said that Athene visited him from time to time, and suggested to him and taught him his laws, and that none of those he promulgated were his own idea and plan.

XII. Perhaps this kind of remedy by talking people over must be contrived for those who are altogether crabbed or envious; but for people of moderation it is not amiss to qualify excessive praise. Thus if anyone should praise you as learned, or rich, or influential, it would be well to bid him not talk about you in that strain, but say that you were good and harmless and useful. For the person that acts so does not introduce his own praise but transfers it, nor does he seem to rejoice in people passing encomiums upon him, but rather to be vexed at their praising him inappropriately and on wrong grounds, and he seems to hide bad traits by better ones, not wishing to be praised, but showing how he ought to be praised. Such seems the intent of such words as the following, "I have not fortified the city with stones or bricks, but if you wish to see how I have fortified it, you will find arms and horses and allies." Still more in point are the last words of Pericles. For as he was dying, and his friends very naturally were weeping and wailing, and reminded him of his military services and his power, and the trophies and victories and towns he had won for Athens,

Even envy is not reluctant to give moderate praise to one that deprecates excessive praise.

People dislike those writers or speakers who entitle themselves wise, but they welcome those who content themselves with saying that they are lovers of philosophy.

and was leaving as a legacy, he raised himself up a little and blamed them as praising him for things common to many, and some of them the results of fortune rather than merit, while they had passed over the best and greatest of his deeds and one peculiarly his own, that he had never been the cause of any Athenian's wearing mourning. This gives the orator an example, if he be a good man, when praised for his eloquence, to transfer the praise to his life and character, and the general who is admired for his skill and good fortune in war to speak with confidence about his gentleness and uprightness. And again, if any very extravagant praise is uttered, such as many people use in flattery which provokes envy, one can reply,

> "I am no god; why do you liken me
> To the immortals?"

If you really know me, praise my integrity, or my sobriety, or my kindheartedness, or my philanthropy. For even envy is not reluctant to give moderate praise to one that deprecates excessive praise, and true panegyric is not lost by people refusing to accept idle and false praise. So those kings who would not be called gods or the sons of gods, but only fond of their brothers or mother, or benefactors, or dear to the gods, did not excite the envy of those that honoured them by those titles, that were noble but still such as men might claim. Again, people dislike those writers or speakers who entitle themselves wise, but they welcome those who content themselves with saying that they are lovers of philosophy, and have made some progress, or use some such moderate language about themselves as that, which does not excite envy. But rhetorical sophists, who expect to hear "Divine, wonderful, grand," at their declamations, are not even welcomed with "Pretty fair, so so."

XIII. Moreover, as people anxious not to injure those who have
weak eyes, draw a shade over too much light, so some people make
their praise of themselves less glaring and absolute, by pointing
out some of their small defects, or miscarriages, or errors, and so
remove all risk of making people offended or envious. Thus
Epeus, who boasts very much of his skill in boxing, and says very
confidently,

> *"I can your body crush, and break your bones,"*

yet says,

> *"Is't not enough that I'm in fight deficient?"*

But Epeus is perhaps a ridiculous instance, excusing his bragging
as an athlete by his confession of timidity and want of manliness.
But agreeable and graceful is that man who mentions his own
forgetfulness, or ignorance, or ambition, or eager desire for
knowledge and conversation. Thus Odysseus of the Sirens,

> *"My heart to listen to them did incline,*
> *I bade my comrades by a nod to unloose me."*

And again of the Cyclops,

> *"I did not hearken (it had been far better),*
> *I wished to see the Cyclops, and to taste*
> *His hospitality."*

And generally speaking the admixture with praise of such faults as
are not altogether base and ignoble stops envy. Thus many have
blunted the point of envy by admitting and introducing, when

*Generally
speaking the
admixture with
praise of such
faults as are
not altogether
base and ignoble
stops envy.*

they have been praised, their past poverty and straits, aye, and their low origin. So Agathocles pledging his young men in golden cups beautifully chased, ordered some earthenware pots to be brought in, and said, "See the fruits of perseverance, labour, and bravery! Once I produced pots like these, but now golden cups." For Agathocles it seems was so low-born and poor that he was brought up in a potter's shop, though afterwards he was king of almost all Sicily.

XIV. These are external remedies against self-praise. There are other internal ones as it were, such as Cato applied, when he said "he was envied, because he had to neglect his own affairs, and lie awake every night for the interests of his country." Compare also the following lines,

> *"How should I boast? who could with ease have been*
> *Enrolled among the many in the army,*
> *And had a fortune equal to the wisest;"*

and,

> *"I shrink from squandering past labours' grace,*
> *Nor do I now reject all present toil."*

Let us consider if we might praise ourselves to excite in our hearers emulation and ambition.

For as it is with house and farm, so also is it with glory and reputation, people for the most part envy those who have got them easily or for nothing, not those who have bought them at the cost of much toil and danger.

XV. Since then we can praise ourselves not only without causing pain or envy but even usefully and advantageously, let us consider, that we may not seem to have only that end in view but some other also, if we might praise ourselves to excite in our hearers emulation and ambition. For Nestor, by reciting his battles and acts of prowess, stirred up Patroclus and nine others to single combat with Hector. For the exhortation that adds deed to word and example and proper emulation is animating and moving and stimulating, and with its impulse and resolution inspires hope that the things we aim at are attainable and not impossible. That is why in the choruses at Lacedæmon the old men sing,

"We once were young and vigorous and strong,"

and then the boys,

"We shall be stronger far than now we are,"

and then the youths,

"We now are strong, look at us if you like."

In this wise and statesmanlike manner did the legislator exhibit to the young men the nearest and dearest examples of what they should do in the persons of those who had done so.

XVI. Moreover it is not amiss sometimes, to awe and repress and take down and tame the impudent and bold, to boast and talk a little big about oneself. As Nestor did, to mention him again,

"For I have mixed ere now with better men
Than both of you, and ne'er did they despise me."

So also Aristotle told Alexander that not only had they that were rulers over many subjects a right to think highly of themselves,

Thus Cyrus talked big in perils and on battle-fields, though at other times he was no boaster.

but also those that had right views about the gods. Useful too against our enemies and foes is the following line,

"Ill-starred are they whose sons encounter me."

Compare also the remark of Agesilaus about the king of the Persians, who was called great, "How is he greater than me, if he is not also more upright?" And that also of Epaminondas to the Lacedæmonians who were inveighing against the Thebans, "Anyhow we have made you talk at greater length than usual." But these kind of remarks are fitting for enemies and foes; but our boasting is also good on occasion for friends and fellow-citizens, not only to abate their pride and make them more humble, but also when they are in fear and dejection to raise them up again and give them confidence. Thus Cyrus talked big in perils and on battle-fields, though at other times he was no boaster. And the second Antigonus, though he was on all other occasions modest and far from vanity, yet in the sea-fight off Cos, when one of his friends said to him, "See you not how many more ships the enemy have got than we have?" answered, "How many do you make me equal to then?" This Homer also seems to have noticed. For he has represented Odysseus, when his comrades were dreadfully afraid of the noise and whirlpool of Charybdis, reminding them of his former cleverness and valour;

"We are in no worse plight than when the Cyclops
By force detained us in his hollow cave;
But even then, thanks to my valour, judgement,
And sense, we did escape."

For such is not the self-praise of a demagogue or sophist, or of one that asks for clapping or applause, but of one who makes his

Such is not the self-praise of a demagogue or sophist, but of one who makes his valour and experience a pledge of confidence to his friends.

valour and experience a pledge of confidence to his friends. For in critical conjunctures the reputation and credit of one who has experience and capacity in command plays a great part in insuring safety.

XVII. As I have said before, to pit oneself against another's praise and reputation is by no means fitting for a public man: however, in important matters, where mistaken praise is injurious and detrimental, it is not amiss to confute it, or rather to divert the hearer to what is better by showing him the difference between true and false merit. Anyone would be glad, I suppose, when vice was abused and censured, to see most people voluntarily keep aloof from it; but if vice should be well thought of, and honour and reputation come to the person who promoted its pleasures or desires, no nature is so well constituted or strong that it would not be mastered by it. So the public man must oppose the praise not of men but of bad actions, for such praise is corrupting, and causes people to imitate and emulate what is base as if it were noble. But it is best refuted by putting it side by side with the truth: as Theodorus the tragic actor is reported to have said once to Satyrus the comic actor, "It is not so wonderful to make an audience laugh as to make them weep and cry." But what if some philosopher had answered him, "To make an audience weep and cry is not so noble a thing as to make them forget their sorrows." This kind of self-laudation benefits the hearer, and changes his opinion. Compare the remark of Zeno in reference to the number of Theophrastus' scholars, "His is a larger body, but mine are better taught." And Phocion, when Leosthenes was still in prosperity, being asked by the orators what benefit he had conferred on the city, replied, "Only this, that during my period of office there has been no funeral oration, but all the dead have

The public man must oppose the praise not of men but of bad actions, for such praise is corrupting.

We must be very much on our guard in praising others not to seem to be really praising ourselves.

been buried in their fathers' sepulchres." Wittily also did Crates parody the lines,

> *"Eating and wantonness and love's delights*
> *Are all I value,"*

with

> *"Learning and those grand things the Muses teach one*
> *Are all I value."*

Such self-praise is good and useful and teaches people to admire and love what is valuable and expedient instead of what is vain and superfluous. Let so much suffice on the question proposed.

XVIII. It remains to me now to point out, what our subject next demands and calls for, how everyone may avoid unseasonable self-praise. For there is a wonderful incentive to talking about oneself in self-love, which is frequently strongly implanted in those who seem to have only moderate aspirations for fame. For as it is one of the rules to preserve good health to avoid altogether places where sickness is, or to exercise the greatest precaution if one must go there, so talking about oneself has its slippery times and places that draw it on on any pretext. For first, when others are praised, as I said before, ambition makes people talk about themselves, and a certain desire and impulse for fame which is hard to check bites and tickles that ambition, especially if the other person is praised for the same things or less important things than the hearer thinks he is a proficient in. For as hungry people have their appetite more inflamed and sharpened by seeing others eat, so the praise of one's neighbours makes those who eagerly desire fame to blaze out into jealousy.

On Contentedness of Mind

XIX. In the second place the narration of things done successfully and to people's mind entices many unawares to boasting and bragging in their joy; for falling into conversation about their victories, or success in state affairs, or their words or deeds commended by great men, they cannot keep themselves within bounds. With this kind of self-laudation you may see that soldiers and sailors are most taken. To be in this state of mind also frequently happens to those who have returned from important posts and responsible duties, for in their mention of illustrious men and men of royal rank they insert the encomiums they have passed on themselves, and do not so much think they are praising themselves as merely repeating the praises of others about themselves. Others think their hearers do not detect them at all of self-praise, when they recount the greeting and welcome and kindness they have received from kings and emperors, but only imagine them to be enumerating the courtesy and kindliness of those great personages. So we must be very much on our guard in praising others to free ourselves from all suspicion of self-love and self-recommendation, and not to seem to be really praising ourselves "under pretext of Patroclus."

He that mixes up his own praise with blame of another, and hunts for fame by defaming another, is altogether tiresome.

XX. Moreover that kind of conversation that mainly consists of censuring and running down others is dangerous as giving opportunity for self-laudation to those who pine for fame. A fault into which old men especially fall, when they are led to scold others and censure their bad ways and faulty actions, and so extol themselves as being remarkably the opposite. In old men we must allow all this, especially if to age they add reputation and merit, for such fault-finding is not without use, and inspires those who are rebuked with both emulation and love of honour. But all other persons must especially avoid and fear that roundabout kind of self-praise. For since generally speaking censuring one's neighbours is disagreeable and barely tolerable and requires great wariness, he that mixes up his own praise with blame of another, and hunts for fame by defaming another, is altogether tiresome and inspires disgust, for he seems to wish to get credit through trying to prove others unworthy of credit.

XXI. Furthermore, as those that are naturally prone and inclined to laughter must be especially on their guard against tickling and touching, such as excites that propensity by contact with the smoothest parts of the body, so those that have a great passion for reputation ought to be especially advised to abstain from praising themselves when they are praised by others. For a person ought to blush when praised, and not to be past blushing from impudence, and ought to check those who extol him too highly, and not to rebuke them for praising him too little; though very many people do so, themselves prompting and reminding their praisers of others of their own acts and virtues, till by their own praise they spoil the effect of the praise that others give them. For some tickle and puff themselves up by self-praise, while others, malignantly holding out the small bait of eulogy, provoke others to talk about themselves, while others again ask questions and put inquiries, as was done to the soldier in Menander, merely to poke fun at him;

Those that have a great passion for reputation ought to be especially advised to abstain from praising themselves when they are praised by others.

> *"'How did you get this wound?' 'Sir, by a javelin.'*
> *'How in the name of Heaven?' 'I was on*
> *A scaling ladder fastened to a wall.'*
> *I show my wound to them in serious earnest,*
> *But they for their part only mock at me."*

XXII. As regards all these points then we must be on our guard as much as possible not to launch out into praise of ourselves, or yield to it in consequence of questions put to us to draw us. And the best caution and security against this is to pay attention to others who praise themselves, and to consider how disagreeable and objectionable the practice is to everybody, and that no other conversation is so offensive and tiring. For though we cannot say that we suffer any other evil at the hands of those who praise themselves, yet being naturally bored by the practice, and avoiding it, we are anxious to get rid of them and breathe again; insomuch that even the flatterer and parasite and needy person in his distress finds the rich man or satrap or king praising himself hard to bear and wellnigh intolerable; and they say that having to listen to all this is paying a very large shot to their entertainment, like the fellow in Menander;

> *"To hear their foolish saws, and soldier talk,*
> *Such as this cursed braggart bellows forth,*
> *Kills me; I get lean even at their feasts."*

For as we may use this language not only about soldiers or men who have newly become rich, who spin us a long yarn of their great and grand doings, being puffed up with pride and talking big about themselves; if we remember that the censure of others always follows our self-praise, and that the end of this vain-glory is a bad repute, and that, as Demosthenes says, the result will be that we shall only tire our hearers, and not be thought what we profess ourselves to be, we shall cease talking about ourselves, unless by so doing we can bestow great benefit on ourselves or our hearers.

Though we cannot say that we suffer any other evil at the hands of those who praise themselves, we are anxious to get rid of them and breathe again.

On Exile.

They say those discourses, like friends, are best and surest that come to our refuge and aid in adversity, and are useful. For many who come forward do more harm than good in the remarks they make to the unfortunate, as people unable to swim trying to rescue the drowning get entangled with them and sink to the bottom together. Now the discourse that ought to come from friends and people disposed to be helpful should be consolation, and not mere assent with a man's sad feelings. For we do not in adverse circumstances need people to weep and wail with us like choruses in a tragedy, but people to speak plainly to us and instruct us, that grief and dejection of mind are in all cases useless and idle and senseless; and that where the circumstances themselves, when examined by the light of reason, enable a man to say to himself that his trouble is greater in fancy than in reality, it is quite ridiculous not to inquire of the body what it has suffered, nor of the mind if it is any the worse for what has happened, but to employ external sympathizers to teach us what our grief is.

II. Therefore let us examine alone by ourselves the weight of our misfortunes, as if they were burdens. For the body is weighed down by the burden of what presses on it, but the soul often adds to the real load a burden of its own. A stone is naturally hard, and

ice naturally cold, but they do not receive these properties and impressions from without; whereas with regard to exile and loss of reputation or honours, as also with regard to their opposites, as crowns and office and position, it is not their own intrinsic nature but our opinion of them that is the gauge of their real joy or sorrow, so that each person makes them for himself light or heavy, easy to bear or hard to bear. When Polynices was asked

"What is't to be an exile? Is it grievous?"

he replied to the question,

"Most grievous, and in deed worse than in word."

Compare with this the language of Alcman, as the poet has represented him in the following lines. "Sardis, my father's ancient home, had I had the fortune to be reared in thee, I should have been dressed in gold as a priest of Cybele, and beaten the fine drums; but as it is my name is Alcman, and I am a citizen of Sparta, and I have learned to write Greek poetry, which makes me greater than the tyrants Dascyles or Gyges." Thus the very same thing one man's opinion makes good, like current coin, and another's bad and injurious.

III. But let it be granted that exile is, as many say and sing, a grievous thing. So some food is bitter, and sharp, and biting to the taste, yet by an admixture with it of sweet and agreeable food we take away its unpleasantness. There are also some colours unpleasant to look at, that quite confuse and dazzle us by their intensity and excessive force. If then we can relieve this by a mixture of shadow, or by diverting the eye to green or some agreeable colour, so too can we deal with misfortunes, mixing

The very same thing one man's opinion makes good, and another's bad and injurious.

up with them the advantages and pleasant things we still enjoy, as wealth, or friends, or leisure, and no deficiency in what is necessary for our subsistence. For I do not think that there are many natives of Sardis who would not choose your fortune even with exile, and be content to live as you do in a strange land, rather than, like snails who have no other home than their shells, enjoy no other blessing but staying at home in ease.

IV. As then he in the comedy that was exhorting an unfortunate friend to take courage and bear up against fortune, when he asked him "how," answered "as a philosopher," so may we also play the philosopher's part and bear up against fortune manfully. How do we do when it rains, or when the North Wind doth blow? We go to the fire, or the baths, or the house, or put on another coat: we don't sit down in the rain and cry. So too can you more than most revive and cheer yourself for the chill of adversity, not standing in need of outward aid, but sensibly using your actual advantages. The surgeon's cupping-glasses extract the worst humours from the body to relieve and preserve the rest of it, whereas the melancholy and querulous by ever dwelling on their worst circumstances, and thinking only of them, and being engrossed by their troubles, make even useful things useless to them, at the very time when the need is most urgent. For as to those two jars, my friend, that Homer says are stored in Heaven, one full of good fortunes, one of bad, it is not Zeus that presides as the dispenser of them, giving to some a gentle and even portion, and to others unmixed streams of evils, but ourselves. For the sensible make their life pleasanter and more endurable by mitigating their sorrows with the consideration of their blessings, while most people, like sieves, let the worst things stick to them while the best pass through.

As to those two jars that Homer says are stored in Heaven, one full of good fortunes, one of bad, it is not Zeus that presides as the dispenser of them, but ourselves.

What part of the whole earth is very far distant from another part, seeing that mathematicians teach us that the whole earth is a mere point compared to heaven?

V. And so, if we fall into any real trouble or evil, we ought to get cheerfulness and ease of mind from the consideration of the actual blessings that are still left to us, mitigating outward trouble by private happiness. And as to those things which are not really evil in their nature, but only so from imagination and empty fancy, we must act as we do with children who are afraid of masks: by bringing them near, and putting them in their hands, and turning them about, we accustom them never to heed them at all: and so we by bringing reason to bear on it may discover the rottenness and emptiness and exaggeration of our fancy. As a case in point let us take your present exile from what you deem your country. For in nature no country, or house, or field, or smithy, as Aristo said, or surgery, is peculiarly ours, but all such things exist or rather take their name in connection with the person who dwells in them or possesses them. For man, as Plato says, is not an earthly and immovable but heavenly plant, the head making the body erect as from a root, and turned up to heaven. And so Hercules said well,

> *"Argive or Theban am I, I vaunt not*
> *To be of one town only, every tower*
> *That does to Greece belong, that is my country."*

But better still said Socrates, that he was not an Athenian or Greek, but a citizen of the world (as a man might say he was a Rhodian or Corinthian), for he did not confine himself to Sunium, or Tænarum, or the Ceraunian mountains.

> *"See you the boundless reach of sky above,*
> *And how it holds the earth in its soft arms?"*

These are the boundaries of our country, nor is there either exile or stranger or foreigner in these, where there is the same fire, water and air, the same rulers, controllers and presidents, the sun the moon and the morning star, the same laws to all, under one appointment and ordinance the summer and winter solstices, the equinoxes, Pleias and Arcturus, the seasons of sowing and planting; where there is one king and ruler, God, who has under his jurisdiction the beginning and middle and end of everything, and travels round and does everything in a regular way in accordance with nature; and in his wake to punish all transgressions of the divine law follows Justice, whom all men naturally invoke in dealing with one another as fellow citizens.

VI. As to your not dwelling at Sardis, that is nothing. Neither do all the Athenians dwell at Colyttus, nor all the Corinthians at Craneum, nor all the Lacedæmonians at Pitane. Do you consider all those Athenians strangers and exiles who removed from Melita to Diomea, where they call the month Metageitnion, and keep the festival Metageitnia to commemorate their migration, and gladly and gaily accept and are content with their neighbourhood with other people? Surely you would not. What part of the inhabited world or of the whole earth is very far distant from another part, seeing that mathematicians teach us that the whole earth is a mere point compared to heaven? But we, like ants or bees, if we get banished from one ant-hill or hive are in sore distress and feel lost, not knowing or having learnt to make and consider all things our own, as indeed they are. And yet we laugh at the stupidity of one who asserts that the moon shines brighter at Athens than at Corinth, though in a sort we are in the same case ourselves, when in a strange land we look on the earth, the sea, the air, the sky, as if we doubted whether or not they were different from those we had been accustomed to. For nature makes us free and unrestrained, but we bind and confine, immure and force ourselves into small and scanty space. Then too

Nature makes us free and unrestrained, but we force ourselves into small and scanty space.

we laugh at the Persian kings, who, if the story be true, drink only of the water of the Choaspes, thus making the rest of the world waterless as far as they are concerned, but when we migrate to other places, we desire the water of the Cephisus, or we yearn for the Eurotas, or Taygetus, or Parnassus, and so make the whole world for ourselves houseless and homeless.

VII. Some Egyptians, who migrated to Ethiopia because of the anger and wrath of their king, to those who begged them to return to their wives and children very immodestly exposed their persons, saying that they would never be in want of wives or children while so provided. It is far more becoming and less low to say that whoever has the good fortune to be provided with the few necessaries of life is nowhere a stranger, nowhere without home and hearth, only he must have besides these prudence and sense, as an anchor and helm, that he may be able to moor himself in any harbour. For a person indeed who has lost his wealth it is not easy quickly to get another fortune, but every city is at once his country to the man who knows how to make it such, and has the roots by which he can live and thrive and get acclimatized in every place, as was the case with Themistocles and Demetrius of Phalerum. The latter after his banishment became a great friend of Ptolemy at Alexandria, and not only passed his days in abundance, but also sent gifts to the Athenians. And Themistocles, who was publicly entertained at the king's expense, is stated to have said to his wife and children, "We should have been ruined, if we had not been ruined." And so Diogenes the Cynic to the person who said to him, "The people of Sinope have condemned you to banishment from Pontus," replied, "And I have condemned them to stay in Pontus, 'by the high cliffs of the inhospitable sea.' " And Stratonicus asked his host at Seriphus, for what offence exile was the appointed

Every city is at once his country to the man who knows how to make it such.

punishment, and being told that they punished rogues by exile, said, "Why then are not you a rogue, to escape from this hole of a place?" For the comic poet says they get their crop of figs down there with slings, and that the island is very barely supplied with the necessaries of life.

VIII. For if you look at the real facts and shun idle fancy, he that has one city is a stranger and foreigner in all others. For it does not seem to such a one fair and just to leave his own city and dwell in another. "It has been your lot to be a citizen of Sparta, see that you adorn your native city," whether it be inglorious, or unhealthy, or disturbed with factions, or has its affairs in disorder. But the person whom fortune has deprived of his own city, she allows to make his home in any he fancies. That was an excellent precept of Pythagoras, "Choose the best kind of life, custom will make it easy." So too it is wise and profitable to say here, "Choose the best and pleasantest city, time will make it your country, and a country that will not always distract you and trouble you and give you various orders such as, 'Contribute so much money, Go on an embassy to Rome, Entertain the prefect, Perform public duties.'" If a person in his senses and not altogether silly were to think of these things, he would prefer to live in exile in some island, like Gryarus or Cinarus,

> *"Savage, and fruitless, ill repaying tillage,"*

and that not in dejection and wailing, or using the language of those women in Simonides,

> *"I am shut in by the dark roaring sea*
> *That foams all round,"*

The sacred governing power of the world enclosed in his breast during all that time never changed its abode.

but he will rather be of the mind of Philip, who when he was thrown in wrestling, and turned round, and noticed the mark his body made in the dust, said, "O Hercules, what a little part of the earth I have by nature, though I desire all the world!"

IX. I think also you have seen Naxos, or at any rate Hyria, which is close here. But the former was the home of Ephialtes and Otus, and the latter was the dwelling-place of Orion. And Alcmæon, when fleeing from the Furies, so the poets tell us, dwelt in a place recently formed by the silting of the Achelous; but I think he chose that little spot to dwell in ease and quiet, merely to avoid political disturbances and factions, and those furies informers. And the Emperor Tiberius lived the last seven years of his life in the island of Capreæ, and the sacred governing power of the world enclosed in his breast during all that time never changed its abode. But the incessant and constant cares of empire, coming from all sides, made not that island repose of his pure and complete. But he who can disembark on a small island, and get rid of great troubles, is a miserable man, if he cannot often say and sing to himself those lines of Pindar, "To love the slender cypress, and to leave the Cretan pastures lying near Ida. I have but little land, where I grow strong, and have nothing to do with sorrow or faction," or the ordinances of princes, or public duties in political emergencies, or state functions hard to get off.

X. For if that seems a good saying of Callimachus, "Do not measure wisdom by a Persian rope," much less should we measure happiness by ropes and parasangs, and if we inhabit an island containing 200 furlongs only, and not (like Sicily) four days' sail round, ought we to wail and lament as if we were very unfortunate? For how does plenty of room bring about an easy life? Have you not heard Tantalus saying in the play,

As to islands Homer seems to sing their praise, and recommend them to us as if on purpose.

On Contentedness of Mind

"I sow a field that takes twelve days to travel round,
The Berecyntian region,"

but shortly after he says,

"My fortunes, that were once as high as heaven,
Now to the ground are fallen, and do say to me,
'Learn not to make too much of earthly things.'"

And Nausithous leaving the spacious Hyperia because of the proximity of the Cyclopes, and migrating to an island "far from all enterprising men," and living an unsocial life,

"Apart from men beside the stormy sea,"

yet contrived to make the life of his citizens very pleasant. And the Cyclades were first inhabited by the sons of Minos, and afterwards by the sons of Codrus and Neleus, though foolish people now think they are punished if they are exiled to them. And yet what island used as a place of exile is not of larger extent than Scillus, where Xenophon after his military service saw a comfortable old age? And the Academy, a small place bought for only 3,000 drachmæ, was the domicile of Plato and Xenocrates and Polemo, who taught and lived there all their lives, except one day every year, when Xenocrates went to Athens to grace the festival of Dionysus, so they said, and to see the new plays exhibited. And Theocritus of Chios twitted Aristotle with loving to live at the courts of Philip and Alexander, and preferring to dwell at the mouth of the Borborus to dwelling in the Academy. For there is a river near Pella that the Macedonians call Borborus. As to islands Homer seems to sing their praise, and recommend them to us as if on purpose, as

When Zeno learned that the only ship he had left was lost at sea, he said, "Fortune, you deal kindly with me, confining me to my threadbare cloak and the life of a philosopher."

The greatest blessing, quiet, which others frequently pant for, you can freely enjoy.

"She came to Lemnos, town of sacred Thoas;"

and,

"What Lesbos has, the seat of the immortals;"

and,

"He captured lofty Scyros, citadel
Of Enyeus;"

and,

"And those who from Dulichium came, and from
The sacred islands called th' Echinades,
That lie across the sea opposite Elis;"

and of the illustrious men that dwelt in islands he mentions Æolus the favourite of the gods, and Odysseus most wise, and Ajax most brave, and Alcinous most kind to strangers.

XI. When Zeno learned that the only ship he had left was with all its freight lost at sea, he said, "Fortune, you deal kindly with me, confining me to my threadbare cloak and the life of a philosopher." And a man not altogether silly, or madly in love with crowds, might, I think, not blame fortune for confining him in an island, but might even praise her for relieving him from weariness and anxiety, and wanderings in foreign countries, and perils by sea, and the uproar of the forum, and for giving him truly a secure, quiet, undistracted and private life, putting him as it were inside a circle in which everything necessary for him was contained. For what island has not a house, a promenade, a bath, and fish and hares for those who love fishing and field-sports?

And the greatest blessing, quiet, which others frequently pant for, you can freely enjoy. And whereas in the world, when men are playing at dice or otherwise enjoying the privacy of their homes, informers and busybodies hunt them up and pursue them from their houses and gardens in the suburbs, and drag them by force to the forum and court, in an island no one comes to bother one or dun one or to borrow money, or to beg one to be surety for him or canvass for him: only one's best friends and intimates come to visit one out of good will and affection, and the rest of one's life is a sort of holy retirement to whoever wishes or has learnt to live the life of leisure. But he who thinks those happy who are always scouring the country, and pass most of their lives in inns and ferryboats, is like a person who thinks the planets happier than fixed stars. And yet every planet keeps its order, rolling in one sphere, as in an island. For, as Heraclitus says, the sun will never deviate from its bounds, for if it did, the Furies, who are the ministers of Justice, would find it out.

He who thinks those happy who are always scouring the country is like a person who thinks the planets happier than fixed stars.

XII. Let us use such and similar language, my friend, and harp upon it, to those who are banished to an island, and are debarred all access with others

"By the sea waves, which many keep apart."

But you who are not tied down to one spot, but only forbidden to live in one, have by that prohibition liberty to go to all others. Moreover to the considerations, I am not in office, or a member of the senate, or an umpire in the games, you may oppose these, I do not belong to any faction, I have no large sums to spend, I have not to dance attendance at the doors of the prefect, it is no odds to me who has got by lot the province, whether he is hot-tempered or an objectionable person. But just as Archilochus overlooked the fruitful fields and vineyards of Thasos, and abused that island as rocky and uneven, and said of it,

"It stands like donkey's chine crowned with wild forest,"

so we, fixing our eyes only on one aspect of exile, its inglorious state, overlook its freedom from cares, its leisure, its liberty. And yet people thought the kings of Persia happy, because they passed their winter in Babylon, their summer in Media, and the pleasant season of spring at Susa. So can the exile be present at the Eleusinian mysteries, at the festival of Dionysus at Athens, at the Nemean games at Argos, at the Pythian games at Delphi, and can pass on and be a spectator of the Isthmian and Corinthian games, if he is fond of sight-seeing; and if not, he has leisure, can walk about, read, sleep without being disturbed, and can say like Diogenes, "Aristotle has to dine when Philip thinks fit, Diogenes can dine at any time he himself chooses," having no business, or magistrate, or prefect, to put him out of his general habits of living.

You will find few of the wisest and most intelligent men buried in their own countries, but most have themselves weighed anchor, and removed.

XIII. And so it is that you will find few of the wisest and most intelligent men buried in their own countries, but most (even without any compulsion) have themselves weighed anchor, and transferred their course, and removed, some to Athens, some from it. For who ever bestowed such encomium upon his country as Euripides did in the following lines?

"First we are not a race brought in from other parts,
But are indigenous, when all other cities
Are, draughts-men like, transferred from place to place,
And are imported from elsewhere. And, lady,
If it is not beside the mark to boast,

We have above us a well-tempered sky,
A climate not too hot, nor yet too cold.
And all the finest things in Greece or Asia
We do procure as an attraction here."

And yet the author of these lines went to Macedonia, and lived all the latter part of his life at the court of Archelaus. And of course you have heard the following epitaph;

"Here lies Euphorion's son, Athenian Æschylus,
To whom death came in corn-producing Gela."

For he, like Simonides before him, went to Sicily. And many have changed the commencing words of Herodotus, "This is the setting forth of the history of Herodotus of Halicarnassus" into "Herodotus of Thurii." For he migrated to Thurii, and participated in that colony. As to the divine and sacred spirit of the Muses, the poet of the Trojan war, Homer, did not many cities claim him as theirs, because he did not cry up one city only? And Hospitable Zeus has many great honours.

XIV. And if anyone shall say that these pursued glory and honour, go to the philosophers, and their schools and lectures, consider those at the Lyceum, the Academy, the Porch, the Palladium, the Odeum. If you admire and prefer the Peripatetic school, Aristotle was a native of Stagira, Theophrastus of Eresus, Strato of Lampsacus, Glyco of Troas, Aristo of Ceos, Critolaus of Phaselis. If you prefer the Stoic school, Zeno was a native of Cittium, Cleanthes of Assus, Chrysippus of Soli, Diogenes of Babylon, Antipater of Tarsus; and the Athenian Archidemus migrated to the country of the Parthians, and left at Babylon a succession of the Stoic school. Who exiled these men? Nobody; it

Who exiled these men? Nobody; it was their own pursuit of quiet, of which no one who is famous or powerful can get much at home.

was their own pursuit of quiet, of which no one who is famous or powerful can get much at home, that made them teach us this by their practice, while they taught us other things by their precepts. And even nowadays most excellent and renowned persons live in strange lands, not in consequence of being expelled or banished, but at their own option, to avoid business and distracting cares, and the want of leisure which their own country would bring them. For it seems to me that the Muses aided our old writers to complete their finest and most esteemed works by calling in exile as a fellow-worker. Thus Thucydides the Athenian wrote the history of the war between the Peloponnesians and the Athenians in Thrace near the forest of Scapte, Xenophon wrote at Scillus in Elis, Philistus in Epirus, Timæus of Tauromenium at Athens, Androtion of Athens at Megara, and Bacchylides the poet in Peloponnesus. All these and many more, though exiled from their country, did not despair or give themselves up to dejection, but so happy was their disposition that they considered exile a resource given them by fortune, whereby they obtained universal fame after their deaths, whereas no memorial is left of those who were factious against them and banished them.

It seems to me that the Muses aided our old writers to complete their finest and most esteemed works by calling in exile as a fellow-worker.

XV. He therefore is ridiculous who thinks that any ignominy attaches itself to exile. What say you? Was Diogenes without glory, whom Alexander saw basking in the sun, and stopped to ask if he wanted anything, and when he answered, "Nothing, but that you would get a little out of my light," Alexander, astonished at his spirit, said to his friends, "If I were not Alexander, I would be Diogenes." Was Camillus without glory when banished from Rome, of which he is now accounted the second founder? And indeed Themistocles did not lose by his exile the glory he had obtained among the Greeks, but he added to it among the barbarians, and there is no one so without honour, so ignoble, who would prefer to be Leobates who indicted him rather than Themistocles the exile, or Clodius who banished Cicero rather than the banished one, or Aristophon the accuser rather than Timotheus who got driven by him from his country.

XVI. But since a good many are moved by the lines of Euripides, who seems to bring a strong indictment against exile, let us see what it is he says in each question and answer about it.

Jocasta. What is't to be an exile? Is it grievous?

Polynices. Most grievous, and in deed worse than in word.

Jocasta. What is its aspect? What is hard for exiles?

Polynices. This is the greatest, that they have no freedom.

Jocasta. This is a slave's life not to speak one's thoughts!

Polynices. Then one must put up with one's masters' follies.

But this is not a right or true estimate. For first of all, not to say out all one thinks is not the action of a slave but of a sensible man, in times and matters that require reticence and silence, as Euripides himself has said elsewhere better,

> *"Be silent where 'tis meet, speak where 'tis safe."*

Then as for the follies of one's masters, one has to put up with them just as much in one's own country as in exile. Indeed, more frequently have the former reason to fear that the powerful in cities will act unjustly to them either through calumny or

As for the follies of one's masters, one has to put up with them just as much in one's own country as in exile.

Nor does exile deprive geometricians or grammarians of their freedom of speech.

violence. But his greatest and absurdest error is that he takes away from exiles freedom of speech. It is wonderful, if Theodorus had no freedom of speech, that when Lysimachus the king said to him, "Did not your country cast you out because of your character?" replied, "Yes, as Semele cast out Dionysus, when unable to bear him any longer." And when he showed him Telesphorus in a cage, with his eyes scooped out, and his nose and ears and tongue cut off, and said to him, "This is how I treat those that act ill to me." And had not Diogenes freedom of speech, who, when he visited Philip's camp just as he was on the eve of offering battle to the Greeks, and was taken before the king as a spy, told him he had come to see his insatiable folly, who was going shortly to stake his dominions and life on a mere die. And did not Hannibal the Carthaginian use freedom of speech to Antiochus, though he was an exile, and Antiochus a king? For as a favourable occasion presented itself he urged the king to attack the enemy, and when after sacrifice he reported that the entrails forbade it, Hannibal chided him and said, "You listen rather to what flesh tells you than to the instruction of a man of experience." Nor does exile deprive geometricians or grammarians of their freedom of speech, or prevent their discussing what they know and have learnt. Why should it then good and worthy men? It is meanness everywhere that stops a man's speech, ties and gags his tongue, and forces him to be silent. But what are the next lines of Euripides?

Jocasta. Hopes feed the hearts of exiles, so they say.

Polynices. Hopes have a flattering smile, but still delay.

But this is an accusation against folly rather than exile. For it is not those who have learnt and know how to enjoy the present, but those who ever hang on the future, and hope after what they have not, that float as it were on hope as on a raft, though they never get beyond the walls.

Jocasta. But did your father's friends do nothing for you?

Polynices. Be fortunate! Friends are no use in trouble.

Jocasta. Did not your good birth better your condition?

Polynices. 'Tis bad to want. Birth brought no bread to me.

But it was ungrateful in Polynices thus to rail against exile as discrediting his good birth and robbing him of friends, for it was on account of his good birth that he was deemed worthy of a royal bride though an exile, and he came to fight supported by a band of friends and allies, a great force, as he himself admits a little later,

Cheseus was an exile from Athens, though it was owing to him that Athens is now inhabited.

> "Many of the princes of the Danai
> And from Mycenæ are with me, bestowing
> A sad but necessary kindness on me."

Nor was there any more justice in the lament of his mother:—

> "I never lit for you the nuptial torch
> In marriage customary, nor did Ismenus
> Furnish you with the usual solemn bath."

She ought to have been pleased and content to hear that her son dwelt in such a palace as that at Argos, and in lamenting that the nuptial torch was not lit, and that he had not had the usual bath in the river Ismenus, as though there was no water or fire at Argos for wedded people, she lays on exile the evils really caused by pride and stupidity.

XVII. But exile, you will say, is a matter of reproach. It may be among fools, who also jeer at the beggar, the bald man, the dwarf, aye, and even the stranger and resident alien. But those who are not carried away in that manner admire good men, whether they are poor, or strangers or exiles. Do we not see that all men adore the temple of Theseus as well as the Parthenon and Eleusinium? And yet Theseus was an exile from Athens, though it was owing to him that Athens is now inhabited, and he was banished from a city which he did not merely dwell in, but had himself built. And what glory is left to Eleusis, if we are ashamed of Eumolpus, who migrated from Thrace, and taught the Greeks (as he still teaches them) the mysteries? And who was the father of Codrus that reigned at Athens? Was it not Melanthus, an exile from Messene? And do you not praise the answer of Antisthenes to the person who told him that his mother was a Phrygian, "So also is the mother of the gods." If you are twitted then with exile, why do you not answer, "The father of the glorious victor Hercules was an exile." And Cadmus, the grandfather of Dionysus, when he was sent from home to find Europa, and never came back, "though a Phoenician born he changed his country," and migrated to Thebes, and became the grandfather of "Dionysus, who rejoices in the cry of Evoe, the exciter of women, who delights in frantic honours." As for what Æschylus obscurely hints at in the line,

The truth is the soul is an exile and wanderer.

"Apollo the chaste god, exile from heaven,"

let me keep a religious silence, as Herodotus says. And Empedocles commences his system of philosophy as follows, "It is an ordinance of necessity, an ancient decree of the gods, when anyone stains his hands with crime and murder, the long-lived demons get hold of him, so that he wanders away from the gods for thirty thousand years. Such is my condition now, that of an exile and wanderer from the gods." In these words he not only speaks of himself, but points out that all of us men similarly are strangers and foreigners and exiles in this world. For he says, "O men, it is not blood or a compounded spirit that made the being or beginning of the soul, but it is your earth-born and mortal body that is made up of these." He calls speciously by the mildest of names the birth of the soul that has come from elsewhere a living in a strange country. But the truth is the soul is an exile and wanderer, being driven about by the divine decrees and laws, and then, as in some sea-girt island, gets joined to the body like an oyster to its shell, as Plato says, because it cannot call to mind or remember from what honour and greatness of happiness it migrated, not from Sardis to Athens, nor from Corinth to Lemnos or Scyros, but exchanging heaven and the moon for earth and life upon earth, if it shifts from place to place for ever so short a time it is put out and feels strange, and fades away like a dying plant. But although one soil is more suitable to a plant than another, and it thrives and grows better on such a soil, yet no situation can rob a man of his happiness or virtue or sense. It was in prison that Anaxagoras wrote his squaring of the circle, and that Socrates, even after drinking the hemlock, talked philosophically, and begged his friends to be philosophers, and was esteemed happy by them. On the other hand, Phaëthon and Tantalus, though they got up to heaven, fell into the greatest misfortunes through their folly, as the poets tell us.

Although one soil is more suitable to a plant than another, and it thrives and grows better on such a soil, yet no situation can rob a man of his happiness.

How One May Be Aware of One's Progress in Virtue.

hat amount of argument, Sossius Senecio, will make a man know that he is improving in respect to virtue, if his advances in it do not bring about some diminution in folly, but vice, weighing equally with all his good intentions, "acts like the lead that makes the net go down?" For neither in music nor grammatical knowledge could anyone recognize any improvement, if he remained as unskilful in them as before, and had not lost some of his old ignorance. Nor in the case of anyone ill would medical treatment, if it brought no relief or ease, by the disease somewhat yielding and abating, give any perception of improvement of health, till the opposite condition was completely brought about by the body recovering its full strength. But just as in these cases there is no improvement unless, by the abatement of what weighs them down till they rise in the opposite scale, they recognize a change, so in the case of those who profess philosophy no improvement or sign of improvement can be supposed, unless the soul lay aside and purge itself of some of its imperfection, and if it continue altogether bad until it become absolutely good and perfect. For indeed a wise man cannot in a moment of time change from absolute badness to perfect goodness, and suddenly abandon for ever all that vice, of which he could not during a long period of time divest himself of

any portion. And yet you know, of course, that those who maintain these views frequently give themselves much trouble and bewilderment about the difficulty, that a wise man does not perceive that he has become wise, but is ignorant and doubtful that in a long period of time by little and little, by removing some things and adding others, there will be a secret and quiet improvement, and as it were passage to virtue. But if the change were so great and sudden that the worst man in the morning could become the best man at night, or should the change so happen that he went to bed vicious and woke up in the morning wise, and, having dismissed from his mind all yesterday's follies and errors, should say,

"False dreams, away, you had no meaning then!"

who on earth could be ignorant of so great a change happening to himself, of virtue blazing forth so completely all at once? I myself am of opinion that anyone, like Cæneus, who, according, to his prayer, got changed from a woman into a man, would sooner be ignorant of the transformation, than that a man should become at once, from a cowardly and senseless person with no powers of self-control, brave and sensible and perfect master of himself, and should in a moment change from a brutish life to a divine without being aware of it.

II. That was an excellent observation, Measure the stone by the mason's rule, not the rule by the stone. But the Stoics, not applying dogmas to facts but facts to their own preconceived opinions, and forcing things to agree that do not by nature, have filled philosophy with many difficulties, the greatest of which is that all men but the perfect man are equally vicious, which has produced the enigma called progress, one little short of extreme

The Stoics produced the enigma called progress.

folly, since it makes those who have not at once under its guidance given up all passions and disorders equally unfortunate as those who have not got rid of a single vile propensity. However they are their own confuters, for while they lay down in the schools that Aristides was as unjust as Phalaris, and Brasidas as great a craven as Dolon, and Plato actually as senseless as Meletus, in life and its affairs they turn away from and avoid one class as implacable, while they make use of the others and trust them in most important matters as most worthy people.

III. But we who see that in every kind of evil, but especially in a disordered and unsettled state of mind, there are degrees of more and less (so that the progress made differs in different cases, badness abating, as a shadow flees away, under the influence of reason, which calmly illuminates and cleanses the soul), cannot consider it unreasonable to think that the change will be perceived, as people who come up out of some ravine can take note of the progress they make upwards. Look at the case from the following point of view first. Just as mariners sailing with full sail over the gaping ocean measure the course they have made by the time they have taken and the force of the wind, and compute their progress accordingly, so anyone can compute his progress in philosophy by his continuous and unceasing course, by his not making many halts on the road, and then again advancing by leaps and bounds, but by his quiet and even and steady march forward guided by reason. For the words of the poet, "If to a little you keep adding a little, and do so frequently, *it will soon be a lot,*" are not only true of the increase of money, but are universally applicable, and especially to increase in virtue, since reason invokes to her aid the enormous force of habit. On the other hand the inconsistencies and dulnesses of some philosophers not only check advance, as it were, on the road, but even break up the

The mathematicians tell us that planets become stationary; but in philosophy there is no such intermission from the cessation of progress.

He who is winged by his zeal and energy cuts through impediments to his progress, as merely obstacles on the road.

journey altogether, since vice always attacks at its leisure and forces back whatever yields to it. The mathematicians tell us that planets, after completing their course, become stationary; but in philosophy there is no such intermission or stationary position from the cessation of progress, for its nature is ever to be moving and, as it were, to be weighed in the scales, sometimes being overweighted by the good preponderating, sometimes by the bad. If, therefore, imitating the oracle given to the Amphictyones by the god, "to fight against the people of Cirrha every day and every night," you are conscious that night and day you ever maintain a fierce fight against vice, not often relaxing your vigilance, or long off your guard, or receiving as heralds to treat of peace the pleasures, or idleness, or stress of business, you may reasonably go forward to the future courageously and confidently.

IV. Moreover, if there be any intermissions in philosophy, and yet your later studies are firmer and more continuous than your former ones, it is no bad indication that your sloth has been expelled by labour and exercise; for the contrary is a bad sign, when after a short time your lapses from zeal become many and continuous, as if your zeal were dying away. For as in the growth of a reed, which shoots up from the ground finely and beautifully to an even and continuous height, though at first from its great intervals it is hindered and baffled in its growth, and afterwards through its weakness is discouraged by any breath of air, and though strengthened by many and frequent joints, yet a violent wind gives it commotion and trembling, so those who at first make great launches out into philosophy, and afterwards find that they are continually hindered and baffled, and cannot perceive that they make any progress, finally get tired of it and cry off. "But he who is as it were winged," is by his simplicity borne along to his end, and by his zeal and energy cuts through impediments to his progress, as merely obstacles on the road. As it is a sign of the growth of violent love, not so much to rejoice in the presence of the loved one, for everyone does that, as to be distressed and grieved at his absence, so many feel a liking for philosophy and seem to take a wonderful interest in the study, but if they are diverted by other matters and business their passion evaporates and they take it very easily. "But whoever is strongly smitten with love for his darling" will show his mildness and agreeableness in the presence of and joint pursuit of wisdom with the loved one, but if he is drawn away from him and is not in his company you will see him in a stew and ill at ease and peevish whether at work or leisure, and unreasonably forgetful of his friends, and wholly impelled by his passion for philosophy. For we ought not to rejoice at discourses only when we hear them, as people like perfumes only when they smell them, and not to seek or care about them in their absence, but in the same condition as people who are hungry and thirsty are in if torn away from food and drink, we ought to follow after true proficiency in philosophy, whether marriage, or wealth, or friendship, or military service, strike in and produce a separation. For just as more is to be got from philosophy, so much the more does what we fail to obtain trouble us.

It is impossible that we should cease to be envious of what most people admire, unless the admiration of virtue was strongly implanted in us.

V. Either precisely the same as this or very similar is Hesiod's very ancient definition of progress in virtue, namely, that the road is no longer very steep or arduous, but easy and smooth and level, its roughness being toned down by exercise, and casting the bright light of philosophy on doubt and error and regrets, such as trouble those who give themselves to philosophy at the outset, like people who leave a land they know, and do not yet descry the land they are sailing to. For by abandoning the common and familiar, before they know and apprehend what is better, they frequently flounder about in the middle and are fain to return. As they say the Roman Sextius, giving up for philosophy all his honours and offices in Rome, being afterwards discontented with philosophy from the difficulties he met with in it at first, very nearly threw himself out of a window. Similarly they relate of Diogenes of Sinope, when he began to be a philosopher, that the Athenians were celebrating a festival, and there were public banquets and shows and mutual festivities, and drinking and revelling all night, and he, coiled up in a corner of the market-place intending to sleep, fell into a train of thought likely seriously to turn him from his purpose and shake his resolution, for he reflected that he had adopted without any necessity a toilsome and unusual kind of life, and by his own fault sat there debarred of all the good things. At that moment, however, they say a mouse stole up and began to munch some of the crumbs of his barley-cake, and he plucked up his courage and said to himself, in a railing and chiding fashion, "What say you, Diogenes? Do your leavings give this mouse a sumptuous meal, while you, the gentleman, wail and lament because you are not getting drunk yonder and reclining on soft and luxurious couches?" Whenever such depressions of mind are not frequent, and the mind when they take place quickly recovers from them, after having put them to flight as it were, and when such annoyance and distraction is easily got rid of, then one may consider one's progress in virtue as a certainty.

VI. And since not only the things that in themselves shake and turn them in the opposite direction are more powerful in the case of weak philosophers, but also the serious advice of friends, and the playful and jeering objections of adversaries bend and soften people, and have ere now shaken some out of philosophy altogether, it will be no slight indication of one's progress in virtue if one takes all this very calmly, and is neither disturbed nor

We would not change virtue for wealth, for while virtue abides, wealth changes hands.

aggravated by people who tell us and mention to us that some of our former comrades are flourishing in kings' courts, or have married wives with dowries, or are attended by a crowd of friends when they come down to the forum to solicit some office or advocateship. He that is not moved or affected by all this is already plainly one upon whom philosophy has got a right hold; for it is impossible that we should cease to be envious of what most people admire, unless the admiration of virtue was strongly implanted in us. For over-confidence may be generated in some by anger and folly, but to despise what men admire is not possible without a true and steady elevation of mind. And so people in such a condition of mind, comparing it with that of others, pride themselves on it, and say with Solon, "We would not change virtue for wealth, for while virtue abides, wealth changes hands, and now one man, now another, has it." And Diogenes compared his shifting about from Corinth to Athens, and again from Thebes to Corinth, to the different residences of the King of Persia, as his spring residence at Susa, his winter residence at Babylon, and his summer residence in Media. And Agesilaus said of the great king, "How is he better than me, if he is not more upright?" And Aristotle, writing to Antipater about Alexander, said, "that he ought not to think highly of himself because he had many subjects, for anyone who had right notions about the gods was entitled to think quite as highly of himself." And Zeno, observing that Theophrastus was admired for the number of his pupils, said, "His choir is, I admit, larger than mine, but mine is more harmonious."

VII. Whenever then, by thus comparing the advantages of virtue with external things, you get rid of envies and jealousies and those things which fret and depress the minds of many who are novices in philosophy, this also is a great indication of your

"His choir is, I admit, larger than mine, but mine is more harmonious."

progress in virtue. Another and no slight indication is a change in the style of your discourses. For generally speaking all novices in philosophy adopt most such as tend to their own glorification; some, like birds, in their levity and ambition soaring to the height and brightness of physical things; others like young puppies, as Plato says, rejoicing in tearing and biting, betake themselves to strifes and questions and sophisms; but most plunging themselves into dialectics immediately store themselves for sophistry; and some collect sentences and histories and go about (as Anacharsis said he saw the Greeks used money for no other purpose but to count it up), merely piling up and comparing them, but making no practical use of them. Applicable here is that saying of Antiphanes, which someone applied to Plato's pupils. Antiphanes said playfully that in a certain city words were frozen directly they were spoken, owing to the great cold, and were thawed again in the summer, so that one could then hear what had been said in the winter. So he said of the words which were spoken by Plato to young men, that most of them only understood them late in life when they were become old men. And this is the condition people are in in respect to all philosophy, until the judgement gets into a sound and healthy state, and begins to adapt itself to those things which can produce character and greatness of mind, and to seek discourses whose footsteps turn inwards rather than outwards, to borrow the language of Æsop. For as Sophocles said he had first toned down the pompous style of Æschylus, then his harsh and over-artificial method, and had in the third place changed his manner of diction, a most important point and one that is most intimately connected with the character, so those who go in for philosophy, when they have passed from flattering and artificial discourses to such as deal with character and emotion, are beginning to make genuine and modest progress in virtue.

Seek discourses whose footsteps turn inwards rather than outwards.

VIII. Furthermore, take care, in reading the writings of philosophers or hearing their speeches, that you do not attend to words more than things, nor get attracted more by what is difficult and curious than by what is serviceable and solid and useful. And also, in studying poems or history, let nothing escape you of what is said to the point, which is likely either to correct the character or to calm the passions. For as Simonides says the bee hovers among the flowers "making the yellow honey," while others value and pluck flowers only for their beauty and fragrance, so of all that read poems for pleasure and amusement he alone that finds and gathers what is valuable seems capable of knowledge from his acquaintance with and friendship for what is noble and good. For those who study Plato and Xenophon only for their style, and cull out only what is pure and Attic, and as it were the dew and the bloom, do they not resemble people who love drugs for their smell and colour, but care not for them as anodynes or purges, and are not aware of those properties? Whereas those who have more proficiency can derive benefit not from discourses only, but from sights and actions, and cull what is good and useful, as is recorded of Æschylus and other similar kind of men. As to Æschylus, when he was watching a contest in boxing at the Isthmus, and the whole theatre cried out upon one of the boxers being beaten, he nudged with his elbow Ion of Chios, and said, "Do you observe the power of training? The beaten man holds his peace, while the spectators cry out." And Brasidas having caught hold of a mouse among some figs, being bitten by it let it go, and said to himself, "Hercules, there is no creature so small or weak that it will not fight for its life!" And Diogenes, seeing a lad drinking water out of the palm of his hand, threw away the cup which he kept in his wallet. So much does attention and assiduous practice make people perceptive and receptive of what contributes to virtue from any source. And this

We must show that we are as willing to listen as to teach.

Neither to be insolent if you come off best in the argument, nor dejected if you come off worst, is a sufficient sign of progress in virtue.

is the case still more with those who mix discourses with actions, who not only, to use the language of Thucydides, "exercise themselves in the presence of danger," but also in regard to pleasures and strifes, and judgements, and advocateships, and magistrateships make a display of their opinions, or rather form their opinions by their practice. For we can no more think those philosophers who are ever learning and busy and investigating what they have got from philosophy, and then straightway publish it in the market-place or in the haunt of young men, or at a royal supper-party, any more than we give the name of physicians to those who sell drugs and mixtures. Nay rather such a sophist differs very little at all from the bird described in Homer, offering his scholars, like the bird, whatever he has got, and as it feeds its callow young from its own mouth, "though it goes ill with itself," so he gets no advantage or food from what he has got for himself.

IX. We must therefore see to it that our discourse be serviceable to ourselves, and that it may not appear to others to be vain-glorious or ambitious, and we must show that we are as willing to listen as to teach, and especially must we lay aside all disputatiousness and love of strife in controversy, and cease bandying fierce words with one another as if we were contending with one another at boxing, and leave off rejoicing more in smiting and knocking down one another than in learning and teaching. For in such cases moderation and mildness, and to commence arguing without quarrelsomeness and to finish without getting into a rage, and neither to be insolent if you come off best in the argument, nor dejected if you come off worst, is a sufficient sign of progress in virtue. Aristippus was an excellent example of this, when overcome in argument by the sophistry of a man, who had plenty of assurance, but was generally speaking mad or half-witted. Observing that he was in great joy and very puffed up at his victory, he said, "I who have been vanquished in the argument shall have a better night's rest than my victor." We can also test ourselves in regard to public speaking, if we are not timid and do not shrink from speaking when a large audience has unexpectedly been got together, nor dejected when we have only a small one to harangue to, and if we do not, when we have to speak to the people or before some magistrate, miss the opportunity through want of proper preparation; for these things are recorded both of Demosthenes and Alcibiades. As for Alcibiades, though he possessed a most excellent understanding, yet from want of confidence in speaking he often broke down, and in trying to recall a word or thought that slipped his memory had to stop short. And Homer did not deny that his first line was unmetrical, though he had sufficient confidence to follow it up by so many other lines, so great was his genius. Much more then ought those who aim at virtue and what is noble to lose no opportunity of public speaking, paying very little attention to either uproar or applause at their speeches.

X. And not only ought each to see to his discourses but also to his actions whether he regards utility more than show, and truth more than display. For if a genuine love for youth or maiden seeks no witnesses, but is content to enjoy its delights privately, far more does it become the philosopher and lover of the beautiful, who is conversant with virtue through his actions, to pride himself on his silence, and not to need people to praise or listen to him. As that man who called his maid in the house, and cried out to her, "See, Dionysia, I am angry no longer," so he that does anything agreeable and polite, and then goes and spreads it about the town, plainly shows that he looks for public applause and has a strong propensity to vain-glory, and as yet has no acquaintance with virtue as a reality but only as a dream, restlessly roving about

Just as in vessels that contain water the air is excluded, so with men that are full of solid merit their pride abates.

amid phantoms and shadows, and making a display of whatever he does as painters display a picture. It is therefore a sign of progress in virtue not merely to have given to a friend or done a good turn to an acquaintance without mentioning it to other people, but also to have given an honest vote among many unjust ones, and to have withstood the dishonourable request of some rich man or of some man in office, and to have been above taking bribes, and, by Zeus, to have been thirsty all night and not to have drunk, or, like Agesilaus, to have resisted, though strongly tempted, the kiss of a handsome youth or maiden, and to have kept the fact to oneself and been silent about it. For one's being satisfied with one's own good opinion and not despising it, but rejoicing in it and acquiescing in it as competent to see and decide on what is honourable, proves that reason is rooted and grounded within one, and that, to borrow the language of Democritus, one is accustomed to draw one's delights from oneself. And just as farmers behold with greater pleasure those ears of corn which bend and bow down to the ground, while they look upon those that from their lightness stand straight upright as empty pretenders, so also among those young men who wish to be philosophers those that are most empty and without any solidity show the greatest amount of assurance in their appearance and walk, and a face full of haughtiness and contempt that looks down on everybody, but when they begin to grow full and get some fruit from study they lay aside their proud and vain bearing. And just as in vessels that contain water the air is excluded, so with men that are full of solid merit their pride abates, and their estimate of themselves becomes a lower one, and they cease to plume themselves on a long beard and threadbare cloak, and transfer their training to the mind, and are most severe and austere to themselves, while they are milder in their intercourse with everybody else; and they do not as before eagerly snatch at the

The more they had to do with learning, the more laying aside their pride and high estimate of themselves.

name and reputation of philosopher, nor do they write themselves down as such, but even if he were addressed by that title by anyone else, an ingenuous young man would say, smiling and blushing, "I am not a god: why do you liken me to the immortals?" For as Æschylus says,

> *"I never can mistake the burning eye*
> *Of the young woman that has once known man,"*

so to the young man who has tasted of true progress in philosophy the following lines of Sappho are applicable, "My tongue cleaves to the roof of my mouth, and a fire courses all over my lean body," and his eye will be gentle and mild, and you would desire to hear him speak. For as those who are initiated come together at first with confusion and noise and jostle one another, but when the mysteries are being performed and exhibited, they give their attention with awe and silence, so also at the commencement of philosophy you will see round its doors much confusion and assurance and prating, some rudely and violently jostling their way to reputation, but he who once enters in, and sees the great light, as when shrines are open to view, assumes another air and is silent and awe-struck, and in humility and decorum follows reason as if she were a god. And the playful remark of Menedemus seems to suit these very well. He said that the majority of those who went to school at Athens became first wise, and then philosophers, after that orators, and as time went on became ordinary kind of people, the more they had to do with learning, so much the more laying aside their pride and high estimate of themselves.

XI. Of people that need the help of the physician some, if their tooth ache or even finger smart, run at once to the doctor, others if they are feverish send for one and implore his assistance at their

Diogenes said that one who wished to do what was right ought to seek either a good friend or red-hot enemy.

own home, others who are melancholy or crazy or delirious will not sometimes even see the doctor if he comes to their house, but drive him away, or avoid him, ignorant through their grievous disease that they are diseased at all. Similarly of those who have done what is wrong some are incorrigible, being hostile and indignant and furious at those who reprove and admonish them, while others are meeker and bear and allow reproof. Now, when one has done what is wrong, to offer oneself for reproof, to expose the case and reveal one's wrongdoing, and not to rejoice if it lies hid, or be satisfied if it is not known, but to make confession of it and ask for interference and admonishment, is no small indication of progress in virtue. And so Diogenes said that one who wished to do what was right ought to seek either a good friend or red-hot enemy, that either by rebuke or mild entreaty he might flee from vice. But as long as anyone, making a display of dirt or stains on his clothes, or a torn shoe, prides himself to outsiders on his freedom from arrogance, and, by Zeus, thinks himself doing something very smart if he jeers at himself as a dwarf or hunchback, but wraps up and conceals as if they were ulcers the inner vileness of his soul and the deformities of his life, as his envy, his malignity, his littleness, his love of pleasure, and will not let anyone touch or look at them from fear of disgrace, such a one has made little progress in virtue, yea rather none. But he that joins issue with his vices, and shows that he himself is even more pained and grieved about them than anyone else, or, what is next best, is able and willing to listen patiently to the reproof of another and to correct his life accordingly, he seems truly to be disgusted at his depravity and resolute to divest himself of it. We ought certainly to be ashamed of and shun every appearance of vice, but he who is more put about by his vice itself than by the bad reputation that ensues upon it, will not mind either hearing it spoken against or even speaking against it himself if it make him a

He who is really making progress in virtue imitates Hippocrates, who confessed publicly that he had made a mistake.

better man. That was a witty remark of Diogenes to a young man, who when seen in a tavern retired into the kitchen: "The more," said he, "you retire, the more are you in the tavern." Even so the more a vicious man denies his vice, the more does it insinuate itself and master him: as those people really poor who pretend to be rich get still more poor from their false display. But he who is really making progress in virtue imitates Hippocrates, who confessed publicly and put into black and white that he had made a mistake about the sutures of the skull, for he will think it monstrous, if that great man declared his mistake, that others might not fall into the same error, and yet he himself for his own deliverance from vice cannot bear to be shown he is in the wrong, and to confess his stupidity and ignorance. Moreover the sayings of Bion and Pyrrho will test not so much one's progress as a greater and more perfect habit of virtue. Bion maintained that his friends might think they had made progress, when they could listen as patiently to abuse as to such language as the following, "Stranger, you look not like a bad or foolish person," "Health and joy go with you, may the gods give you happiness!" While as to Pyrrho they say, when he was at sea and in peril from a storm, that he pointed out a little pig that was quietly enjoying some grain that had been scattered about, and said to his companions that the man who did not wish to be disturbed by the changes and chances of life should attain a similar composedness of mind through reason and philosophy.

XII. Look also at the opinion of Zeno, who thought that everybody might gauge his progress in virtue by his dreams, if he saw himself in his dreams pleasing himself with nothing disgraceful, and neither doing nor wishing to do anything dreadful or unjust, but that, as in the clear depths of a calm and tranquil sea, his fancy and passions were plainly shown to be

Lamentations in the case of sad and strange dreams are like the waves that break on the coast, the soul not having yet got its proper composure.

There is no ardent and energetic praise of virtue which does not prick and goad one on to do something similar.

under the control of reason. And this had not escaped the notice of Plato, it seems, who had earlier expressed in form and outline the part that fancy and unreason played in sleep in the soul that was by nature tyrannical, "for it attempts incest," he says, "with its mother, and procures for itself unlawful meats, and gives itself up to the most abandoned desires, such as in daytime the law through shame and fear debars people from." As then beasts of burden that have been well-trained do not, even if their driver let go the reins, attempt to turn aside and leave the proper road, but go forward orderly as usual, pursuing their way without stumbling, so those whose unreason has become obedient and mild and tempered by reason, will not easily wish, either in dreams or in illnesses, to deal insolently or lawlessly through their desires, but will keep to their usual habits, which acquire their power and force by attention. For if the body can by training make itself and its members so subject to control, that the eyes in sorrow can refrain from tears, and the heart from palpitating in fear, and the passions can be calm in the presence of beautiful youths and maidens, is it not far more likely that the training of the passions and emotions of the soul will allay, tame down, and mould their propensities even in dreams? A story is told about the philosopher Stilpo, that he thought he saw in a dream Poseidon angry with him because he had not sacrificed an ox to him, as was usual among the Megarians: and that he, not a bit frightened, said, "What are you talking about, Poseidon? Do you come here as a peevish boy, because I have not with borrowed money filled the town with the smell of sacrifice, and have only sacrificed to you out of what I had at home on a modest scale?" Then he thought that Poseidon smiled at him, and held out his right hand, and said that for his sake he would give the Megarians a large shoal of anchovies. Those, then, that have such pleasant, clear, and painless dreams, and no frightful, or harsh, or malignant, or untoward apparition, may be said to have reflections of their progress in virtue; whereas agitation and panics and ignoble flights, and boyish delights, and lamentations in the case of sad and strange dreams, are like the waves that break on the coast, the soul not having yet got its proper composure, but being still in course of being moulded by opinions and laws, from which it escapes in dreams as far as possible, so that it is once again set free and open to the passions. Do you investigate all these points too, as to whether they are signs of progress in virtue, or of some habit which has already a settled constancy and strength through reason.

XIII. Now since entire freedom from the passions is a great and divine thing, and progress in virtue seems, as we say, to consist in a certain remissness and mildness of the passions, we must observe the passions both in themselves and in reference to one another to gauge the difference: in themselves as to whether desire, and fear, and rage are less strong in us now than formerly, through our quickly extinguishing their violence and heat by reason; and in reference to one another as to whether we are animated now by modesty more than by fear, and by emulation more than by envy, and by love of glory rather than by love of riches, and generally speaking whether—to use the language of musicians—it is in the Dorian more than in the Lydian measures that we err either by excess or deficiency, whether we are plainer in our manner of living or more luxurious, whether we are slower in action or quicker, whether we admire men and their discourses more than we should or despise them. For as it is a good sign in diseases if they turn aside from vital parts of the body, so in the case of people who are making progress in virtue, when vice seems to shift to milder passions, it is a sign it will soon die out. When Phrynis added to the seven chords two chords more, the Ephors

It is a special sign of true progress in virtue to love and admire the disposition of those whose deeds we emulate.

asked him which he preferred to let them cut off, the upper or lower ones; so we must cut off both above and below, if we mean to attain, to the mean and to due proportion: for progress in virtue first diminishes the excess and sharpness of the passions,

"That sharpness for which madmen are so vehement,"

as Sophocles says.

XIV. I have already said that it is a very great indication of progress in virtue to transfer our judgement to action, and not to let our words remain merely words, but to make deeds of them. A manifestation of this is in the first place emulation as regards what we praise, and a zeal to do what we admire, and an unwillingness either to do or allow what we censure. To illustrate my meaning by an example, it is probable that all Athenians praised the daring and bravery of Miltiades; but Themistocles alone said that the trophy of Miltiades would not let him sleep, but woke him up of a night, and not only praised and admired him, but manifestly emulated and imitated his glorious actions. Small, therefore, can we think the progress we have made, as long as our admiration for those who have done noble things is barren, and does not of itself incite us to imitate them. For as there is no strong love without jealousy, so there is no ardent and energetic praise of virtue, which does not prick and goad one on, and make one not envious but emulous of what is noble, and desirous to do something similar. For not only at the discourses of a philosopher ought we, as Alcibiades said, to be moved in heart and shed tears, but the true proficient in virtue, comparing his own deeds and actions with those of the good and perfect man, and grieved at the same time at the knowledge of his own deficiency, yet rejoicing in hope and desire, and full of impulses that will not let him rest, is, as

Whoever is steeped in envy against his betters, let him know that he neither honours nor admires virtue.

On Contentedness of Mind

Simonides says,

"Like sucking foal running by side of dam,"

being desirous all but to coalesce with the good man. For it is
a special sign of true progress in virtue to love and admire the
disposition of those whose deeds we emulate, and to resemble
them with a goodwill that ever assigns due honour and praise to
them. But whoever is steeped in contentiousness and envy
against his betters, let him know that he may be pricked on by a
jealous desire for glory or power, but that he neither honours nor
admires virtue.

XV. Whenever, then, we begin so much to love good men that we
deem happy, "not only," as Plato says, "the temperate man himself,
but also the man who hears the words that flow from his wise
lips," and even admire and are pleased with his figure and walk and
look and smile, and desire to adapt ourselves to his model and to
stick closely to him, then may we think that we are making genuine
progress. Still more will this be the case, if we admire the good not
only in prosperity, but like lovers who admire even the lispings and
paleness of those in their flower, as the tears and dejection of
Panthea in her grief and affliction won the affections of Araspes, so
we fear neither the exile of Aristides, nor the prison of Anaxagoras,
nor the poverty of Socrates, nor the condemnation of Phocion, but
think virtue worthy our love even under such trials, and join her,
ever chanting that line of Euripides,

"Unto the noble everything is good."

For the enthusiasm that can go so far as not to be discouraged at
the sure prospect of trouble, but admires and emulates what is

*The enthusiasm
that can go so
far as not to be
discouraged at
the sure prospect
of trouble could
never be turned
away from
what is noble.*

good even so, could never be turned away from what is noble by anybody. Such men ever, whether they have some business to transact, or have taken upon them some office, or are in some critical conjuncture, put before their eyes the example of noble men, and consider what Plato would have done on the occasion, what Epaminondas would have said, how Lycurgus or Agesilaus would have dealt; that so, adjusting and re-modelling themselves, as it were, at their mirrors, they may correct any ignoble expression, and repress any ignoble passion. For as those that have learnt the names of the Idæan Dactyli make use of them to banish their fear by quietly repeating them over, so the bearing in mind and remembering good men, which soon suggests itself forcibly to those who have made some progress in virtue in all their emotions and difficulties, keeps them upright and not liable to fall. Let this also then be a sign to you of progress in virtue.

XVI. In addition to this, not to be too much disturbed, nor to blush, nor to try and conceal oneself, or make any change in one's dress, on the sudden appearance of a man of distinction and virtue, but to feel confident and go and meet such a one, is the confirmation of a good conscience. It is reported that Alexander, seeing a messenger running up to him full of joy and holding out his right hand, said, "My good friend, what are you going to tell me? Has Homer come to life again?" For he thought that his own exploits required nothing but posthumous fame. And a young man improving in character instinctively loves nothing better than to take pride and pleasure in the company of good and noble men, and to display his house, his table, his wife, his amusements, his serious pursuits, his spoken or written discourses; insomuch that he is grieved when he remembers that his father or guardian died without seeing him in that condition in life, and would pray for nothing from the gods so much, as that they could come to life

Alexander thought that his own exploits required nothing but posthumous fame.

again, and be spectators of his life and actions; as, on the contrary, those that have neglected their affairs, and come to ruin, cannot look upon their relatives even in dreams without fear and trembling.

XVII. Add, if you please, to what I have already said, as no small indication of progress in virtue, the thinking no wrong-doing small, but being on your guard and heed against all. For as people who despair of ever being rich make no account of small expenses, thinking they will never make much by adding little to little, but when hope is nearer fruition, then with wealth increases the love of it, so in things that have respect to virtue, not he that generally assents to such sayings as "Why trouble about hereafter?" "If things are bad now, they will some day be better," but the man who pays heed to everything, and is vexed and concerned if vice gets pardon, when it lapses into even the most trifling wrongdoing, plainly shows that he has already attained to some degree of purity, and deigns not to contract defilement from anything whatever. For the idea that we have nothing of any importance to bring disgrace upon, makes people inclined to what is little and careless. To those who are building a stone wall or coping it matters not if they lay on any chance wood or common stone, or some tombstone that has fallen down, as bad workmen do, heaping and piling up pell-mell every kind of material; but those who have made some progress in virtue, whose life "has been wrought on a golden base," like the foundation of some holy or royal building, undertake nothing carelessly, but lay and adjust everything by the line and level of reason, thinking the remark of Polycletus superlatively good, that that work is most excellent, where the model stands the test of the nail.

That work is most excellent, where the model stands the test of the nail.

193

Uncommon Books
for Serious Readers

A Fortnight in the Wilderness
Alexis de Tocqueville

Gnomologia—1732
The proverbs that inspired
Benjamin Franklin

The Grimani Breviary
Foreword by Ross King

The Happy Warrior
The life story of Sir Winston
Churchill as told through the
Eagle comic of the 1950s

**Jerusalem: The Saga of
the Holy City**
Benjamin Mazar et al.

**John F. Kennedy: The Making of
His Inaugural Address**
Commentary by Roger G. Kennedy

**The Little Guide to Your
Well-Read Life**
Steve Leveen

The Making of The Finest Hour
Speech by Winston S. Churchill
Introduction by
Richard M. Langworth

Notes on Our Times
E. B. White

On a Life Well Spent
Cicero
Preface by Benjamin Franklin

On Becoming Abraham Lincoln
John T. Morse Jr., 1893

Painting as a Pastime
Winston S. Churchill

Samuel Johnson's Dictionary
Selections from the 1755 work
that defined the English language
Edited by Jack Lynch

The Sarajevo Haggadah
Authorized facsimile of the
14th-century original

The Silverado Squatters
Six selected chapters
Robert Louis Stevenson

**Sir Winston Churchill's Life
Through His Paintings**
David Coombs
with Minnie Churchill
Foreword by Mary Soames

Levenger Press is the publishing arm of

Levengerpress.com   800.544.0880

To write your review of this book or any Levenger Press title,
please visit Levenger.com and type the book title into the Search box.